Study Guide and Workbook

WESTERN HERITAGE BRIEF

Volume I: To 1715

Donald Kagan
YALE UNIVERSITY

Steven Ozment
HARVARD UNIVERSITY

Frank M. Turner
YALE UNIVERSITY

Prepared by
Anthony M. Brescia
Department of History
NASSAU COMMUNITY COLLEGE

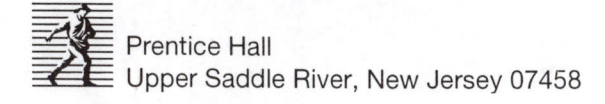

Prentice Hall
Upper Saddle River, New Jersey 07458

© 1996 by PRENTICE-HALL, INC.
Simon and Schuster/A Viacom Company
Upper Saddle River, New Jersey 07458

All rights reserved

10 9 8 7 6 5 4 3 2 1

ISBN 0-13-466806-5
Printed in the United States of America

VOLUME I

Chapter		Page
1	The World Before the West	1
2	The Rise of Greek Civilization	10
3	Classical and Hellenistic Greece	20
4	Rome: From Republic to Empire	31
5	The Roman Empire	40
	Further Consideration from Chapters 1 — 5	50
6	The Early Middle Ages (476-1000): The Birth of Europe	51
7	The High Middle Ages (1000-1300): The Ascendancy of the Church and the Rise of States	60
8	The High Middle Ages (1000-1300): People, Towns and Universities	69
9	The Late Middle Ages (1300-1527): Centuries of Crisis	78
10	Renaissance and Discovery	87
	Further Consideration from Chapters 6 — 10	97
11	The Age of Reformation	98
12	The Age of Religious Wars	108
13	Paths to Constitutionalism and Absolutism: England and France in the Seventeenth Century	118
14	New Directions in Thought and Culture in the Sixteenth and Seventeenth Centuries	127
15	Successful and Unsuccessful Paths to Power (1686-1740)	136
	Further Consideration from Chapters 11 — 15	145

INTRODUCTION

WELCOME to the Brief edition of the *Guide*. Users of this study tool will find the sections updated and corresponding to the *Western Heritage Brief*. Note that while the "Further Consideration" sections have been preserved, those corresponding to the original documents presented in each chapter are now located at the end of every fifth chapter of the *Guide*.

Generally defined, history is learning about humankind's continuing experience by inquiry. It is the process of asking questions about things that have happened, are happening, and are likely to happen in the future. History deals with the essence of being human. It is one of the studies that most clearly separates the human species from all others. From the very beginning of human development peoples have asked, "What's happening'?" Why have they done so? What is it about us that causes the questions to be asked? It is the human species, collectively, and each of us alone that has the capacity to think and reason beyond the present. To be human is to be historical. No other creature is endowed with the ability to consider time and space, what has gone before and what will come after. To understand civilization one must also contemplate death. You and I are among the only animals of the earth who early in life must come to grips with the inevitability of our own mortality. So that we may each better understand these realities the study of history has become the structured process that is organized to reflect the growth of civilizations and the development of their human cargo.

No matter what is said about the study of history, our understanding of the past remains the core of a liberal arts education, the mark of an educated person, and an essential adjunct to our lives, regardless of career choice. This is true because many of the methods used to learn about the past are similar to the skills we use to understand the present. We are, in fact, doing little more than very carefully and thoughtfully reading the newspaper of today's past. By so doing, and by drawing on the skills of the text writers, we are seeking an enlightened, manageable, and comprehensible view of what has been.

The study of history is both a joy and a discipline. It is a joy because it brings into our lives much of the fascinating past. Yet, because there is so much of that past available to us, historical research or study can be a chore, although it need not be.

This edition of the *Guide is* designed to serve students seeking a better understanding of their own heritage within that of the West. It can be used to improve one's grade and also one's overall study skills. Any student, whatever his or her ability, will benefit from the commentary and exercises provided. The *Guide is* another means by which your instructor, the authors of the textbook, and this workbook, hope to guide you through this study of the past.

As noted below, the chapter related exercises are designed to reinforce the historical ideas and thoughts presented within each chapter of the textbook. Attention is also called to historical persons and events that are essential to understanding the fabric of the past. Virtually all chapters include map exercises. A series of questions that draw closer attention to the documents will be found after every fifth chapter of the *Guide*.

Designed as a supplement to the text, this volume can be used to gain an overall view of a particular chapter, and to call attention to selected items of historical importance within each chapter. The use of this *Guide* also provides an opportunity to test yourself on the material you have read in each chapter. These short-answer-type questions are of a kind commonly found and increasingly utilized at various levels of our educational system and in many subject areas. These questions are intended to sharpen your understanding of the chapter and to help in the comprehension of the historic data, whereas the essay questions are aimed at encouraging thought and an understanding of the larger concepts developed within each chapter. Map exercises are provided so that places and their importance in the historical picture are not lost. Continued attention has been given to physical geography in this edition. The *Guide* is arranged by chapters that correspond to those of the text. As in previous editions the page numbers corresponding to the textbook are appropriately provided throughout. Within each chapter of this Guide you will find the following:

COMMENTARY

A brief overview that highlights the development of each chapter, this section is intended to present an overall understanding of the chapter. You should read this section for a preview and later as a review of the text material.

IDENTIFICATIONS [HISTORICAL]

These are a selection of notable terms, places, events, and persons that are introduced in the chapter. *It should he noted that these identifications are only a selected sample.* They are designed to call your attention to those historical factors that are beyond the obvious and therefore appear to be of lesser importance. Use this section to deepen your understanding of specific items within each chapter.

MAP EXERCISES

These exercises, marked A and B, are intended to familiarize you with the geography and the location of important places, events, and boundaries within a specific region or wider area. Some of these exercises will require you to consult other sources or an atlas.

SHORT-ANSWER EXERCISES

The multiple-choice, true-false, and completion questions are designed to help you check on specific points and ideas developed within the chapter. These questions are not intended to be difficult, and you should be able to answer them after a reasonably careful study of the chapter. The correct answers are provided at the end of each chapter, along with the appropriate page references to *The Western Heritage Brief*.

FOR FURTHER CONSIDERATION

These essay questions are aimed at provoking thought about the wider concepts and historical problems raised within each chapter; BUT are generally different than those found at the end of each chapter of the text itself.

And grouped after every five chapters,

FOR FURTHER CONSIDERATION OF THE DOCUMENTS:

These essay questions are designed to provoke some thoughtful analysis respective to the special, boxed documents presented in the previous five chapters. Page numbers are provided as a reference back to these documents. These questions are generally different than those found in the document section of the text itself.

THE WORLD BEFORE THE WEST

COMMENTARY

The abilities to think abstractly and to mold our environment are the basic and most important distinguishing characteristics of being human. The early stages of human development are readily outlined, and the transition from hunter-gatherer to food producer can be followed. The movement of peoples into the river valleys of the ancient Near East was a primary stimulus to the formation of cities. Here these early peoples developed and expanded their civilization, building skills in writing, division of labor, smelting of metals, and basic organizational techniques. Soon these riverine civilizations were politically unified, producing a central administration, powerful monarchs, and rigid class systems.

Mesopotamia, "the land between the rivers," is the first of the river valleys to undergo this transformation. The first monarch successfully to rule there was the Semite king Sargon. Semite descendants of Sargon, having conquered the Sumerians for two centuries from the middle of the twenty-fourth century B.C., ruled until internal weakness and foreign attack swept them aside. In 1900 B.C. another Semitic group, the Amorites, came to control the Babylonian state. Autocratic, religiously centered, and class-, if not caste-, structured, they ruled the Mesopotamian state. To other symbols of success developing at this time, such as a written system of wedge-shaped *cuneiform* characters and an advanced mathematical system, the Amorite King Hammurabi added a written legal system. Interestingly, it is the modern knowledge of this legal document that yields considerable insight to everyday life in those times. Since the Code of Hammurabi attempted to regulate many aspects of Mesopotamian society, it remains a valuable tool for understanding ancient peoples and their life-styles. Within this well-organized state-religious government, large numbers of scribes were kept busy keeping records for civil and godly purposes. This Mesopotamian religious culture gave rise to the architectural achievement of the ziggurats, some of which can still be visited today were it not for the current instability of the region.

By contrast to the chaotic history and less certain climate of Mesopotamia, the civilization of ancient Egypt developed in an almost serene setting. In a land isolated from the rest of the world by sea and desert and joined by the length of the Nile, the ancient Egyptians looked optimistically to the future. The relative stability of Egyptian life from the first pharaoh, Menes, to the conquest of Alexander the Great almost three thousand years later is demonstrated through the long dynastic history of the country. Despite foreign invasion and much internal turbulence, succeeding dynasties and kingdoms were able to reassert themselves. Not unrelated to Egypt's stability is the emphasis upon religious life, particularly the afterlife. The gods dominated all aspects of life and the sun god Re dominated all the gods. The Egyptian belief centered on the reality of achieving immortality. Hence the elaborate means through which the body and thereby the soul were to be preserved: embalming, mummification, pyramids, proper prayers and spells, and eventually a test of morality.

Though ancient Egypt eventually weakened, there was little slowing in the constant struggles for supremacy among the peoples of the region. A series of successful states under the Hyksos, Hittites, Kassites, Mitannians, and Assyrians all held influence for various periods in the ancient Near East. Despite their respective ascendancy these peoples had little lasting effect on the future development of Western civilization. By the middle of the sixth century B.C. they were eclipsed by the rising power of Persia, modern Iran.

The greatest influence from this period on Western civilization did not come from the powerful and prolonged kingdoms of Mesopotamia and Egypt or from the warlike successor states that from time to time held sway in the area, but rather from a group that came to inhabit a part of early Palestine. That influence developed from a comparatively small group of people whose existence would have passed unnoticed were it not for the uniqueness of their religious belief and practice. The uncompromising faith and loyalty of the Israelites, the people of the Kingdom of Judah, the Jews, to monotheism and the laws of Moses have reached across time and space as a central contribution to the Western heritage.

The literature of these times, like that of any era, truly reflects the concerns and fears of the people. Faced with the powers of nature and uncertain of their own future, the people through their literature denoted the birth and rise of the gods to preeminence, and the corresponding helplessness of being human. Babylonian and Egyptian tales and legends stress the powers of the supernatural. Individuals, or an entire people, could struggle to please the gods through a series of prescribed formulas. But they could never be assured that the gods were listening, or even willing to help. It is not until the advent of the Greek philosophical tradition after the sixth century B.C. that human beings will seek to understand more about their condition. Relying less on the gods they will begin to explore the secrets of nature by drawing upon their own abstract abilities. With the early Greek thinkers an extraordinary intellectual transition begins as human beings turn to reason and science to learn the mysteries and substance of life.

IDENTIFICATIONS

Chapter 1: The World Before the West

Identify each one of the following as used in the text. Refer to the text as necessary.

	Text Page
Homo Sapiens	2
culture	2
Sumerians	5
Semitic languages	5
Hammurabi	6
cuneiform	6
ziggurat	7
Enlil	9
nomes	12
Hyksos	13
Osiris	13
Aton	13-15
General Horemhab	15
The Book of the Dead	13-15
Hittites	16
Islam	17
Abraham	17
King Nebuchadnezzar II	18
"cattle of god"	20
Thales	21
Hippocrates of Cos	21

Map Exercise A

Outline and/or locate each of the following on the accompanying map:

1. land of Egypt
2. Nile River
3. Tigris River
4. Euphrates River
5. Mesopotamia/Babylonia
6. Phoenicia
7. kingdom of Israel
8. kingdom of Judah
9. kingdom of the Hittites
10. Greece
11. Crete
12. Cyprus
13. Thrace
14. Mt. Sinai

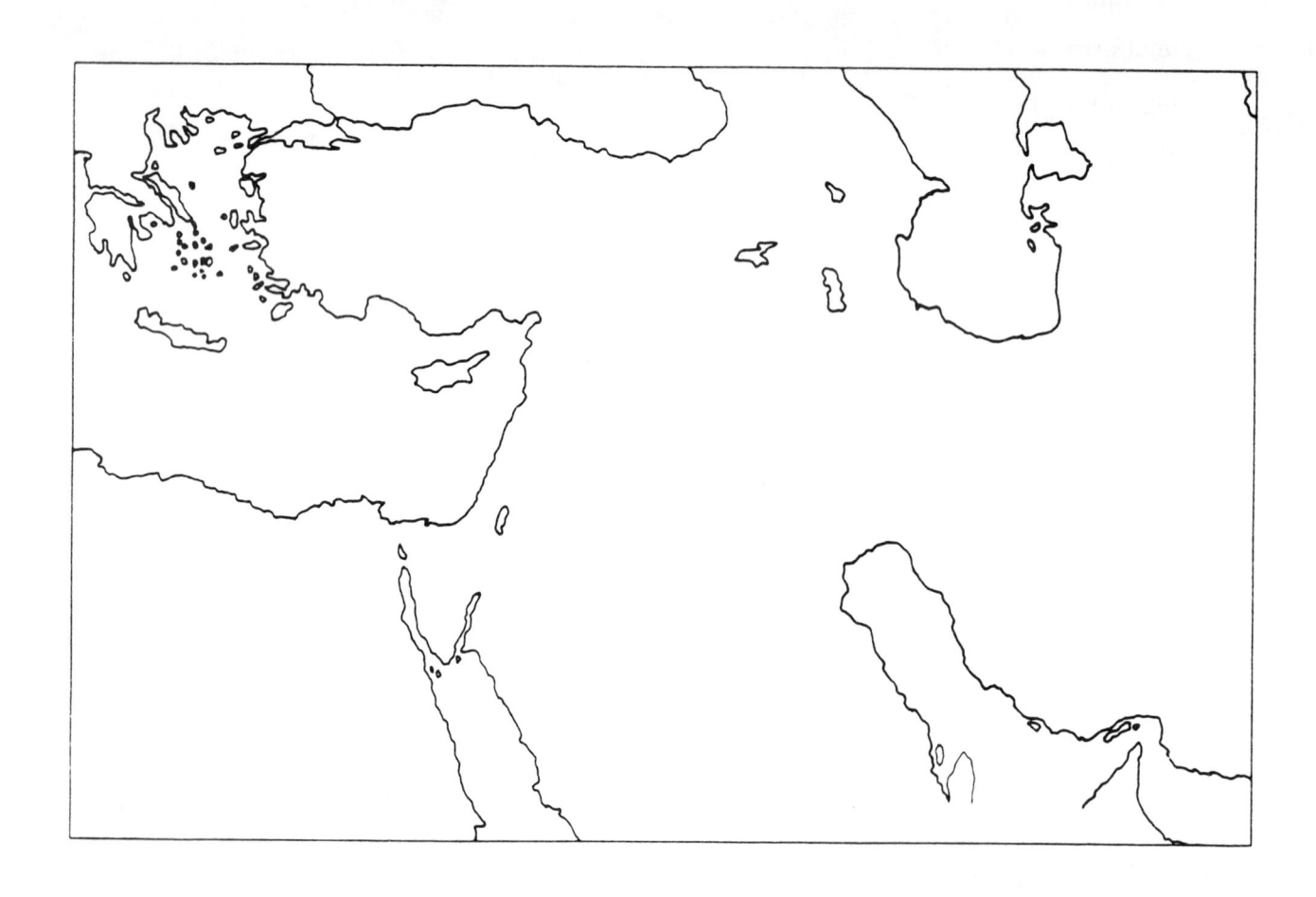

Map Exercise B

Using the same outline map provided in Exercise A, locate the boundaries or partial boundaries of all the modern countries touched by this map.

Additionally, properly identify and locate the more prominent bodies of water, rivers, mountains, and islands.

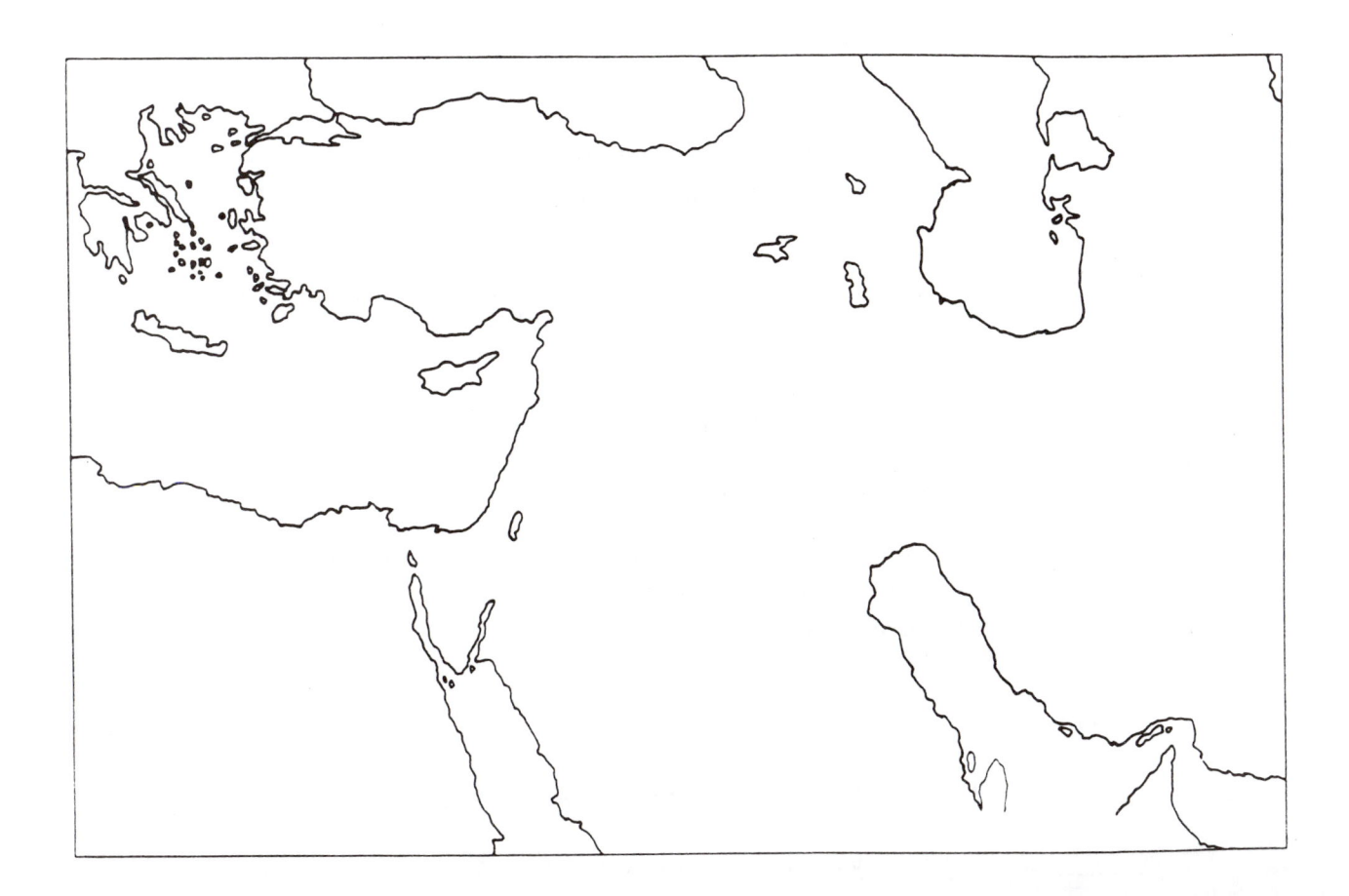

5
CHAPTER 1
THE WORLD BEFORE
THE WEST

Short-Answer Exercises

Multiple-Choice

~~B~~ C 1. The culture of early human beings shows that much trust was placed in: (a) wild beasts, (b) their ancestors, (c) religion and magic, (d) natural disasters.

A 2. Division of labor between the sexes appears to have initiated through the manner of: (a) obtaining different foodstuffs, (b) making tools and weapons, (c) making clothing, (d) child-bearing.

D 3. The so-called Neolithic Revolution clearly produced: (a) increased disease, (b) a decline in world population, (c) a dramatic increase in world population, (d) the pre-conditions for the emergence of civilization.

___C___ 4. Which of the following was probably <u>not</u> among the first known uses of writing: (a) to record the behavior of rivers, (b) to list the possessions of kings and temples, (c) to map streets of early capital cities, (d) to record laws and acts of government.

B / A or C / ~~A~~ 5. The earliest Mesopotamian kingdoms were commonly ruled by: (a) popular generals, (b) priest-kings, (c) local assemblies, (d) scribes.

___D___ 6. The pyramids of Egypt are an invaluable source of information about that civilization for they indicate: (a) great technical skill, (b) the extent of royal power, (c) the enormous wealth of the pharaoh, (d) all of these.

C / ~~B~~ 7. *Hieroglyphics*, the sacred writing of ancient Egypt: (a) were only carved inside the pyramids, (b) were designed to record the bounty of harvests and trade, (c) lacked the depth, imagination and seriousness of Mesopotamian literature, (d) were purely mathematical in scope.

B / ~~a~~ 8. The peoples of the ancient Near East especially noted for their cruelty and brutality were the: (a) Mitannians, (b) Assyrians, (c) Hittites, (d) Phoenicians.

___A___ 9. The end of the Babylonian Captivity of the Jews occurred when: (a) the Jews were released from bondage in Babylon by the Persians, (b) Moses led his people out of Egypt, (c) the state of Israel was formed in 1948, (d) Jews abandoned their belief in a Messiah.

___D___ 10. Ancient literature appears to suggest that the function of mankind is to: (a) understand the gods, (b) develop their own lives, (c) control nature, (d) serve the gods.

True/False

_____ 1. The Neolithic economy appears based upon the cultivation of wheat.

_____ 2. A centrally planned economy was a key factor of Mesopotamian life.

_____ 3. As far as can be known, Mesopotamian wives were legally able to seek a divorce.

_____ 4. Mesopotamian slavery was principally designed as punishment for the poor behavior of teenagers.

_____ 5. Throughout Egyptian history the god Aton was of singular importance.

_____ 6. Surprisingly, the tomb of the pharaoh Tutankhamon was not discovered until 1922.

_____ 7. The Mediterranean trading cities of the Phoenicians helped transmit culture from east to west.

_____ 8. The Hebrew prophetic tradition asserted that God would redeem His people and restore the House of David through the coming of Jesus Christ.

_____ 9. God saved Noah because of his ship building skills.

_____ 10. Hippocrates believed that all diseases could be found to have a supernatural cause.

Completion

1. The _____ Revolution could also be referred to as the Age of Agriculture.

2. The first civilization founded in Mesopotamia was that of the _____.

3. The first ruling dynasty of Sumer and Akkad developed from the king _____.

4. _____ was one of the great heroes to emerge in the poetic literature of ancient Mesopotamia.

5. The Eighteenth Dynasty of Egypt saw an interesting religious revolt led by the pharaoh _____.

6. The modern religions of Judaism, Christianity, and Islam have their origins in the area of _____.

7. _____ were an important trading people who had developed a simplified writing system.

8. The greatest contribution of the Jews in the area of religion is their acceptance of _____.

9. According to one Egyptian legend, the god Re, though relenting, once attempted to destroy humanity through the goddess _____.

10. _____ was the first Greek philosopher.

FOR FURTHER CONSIDERATION

1. Describe the movement of early Neolithic peoples to the river-watered lowlands. What caused this movement? What factors were operating that brought about the rise of cities in these river valleys?

2. From your perspective, how does the law code of Hammurabi relate to established principles of law in the Western world today? How do you think the code would deal with current legal issues and problems?

3. What were the fundamental beliefs of the ancient Hebrews'? How have these beliefs affected the later religions of Christianity and Islam'?

4. Judging by ancient literary examples, how did the people of that time view the relationship between the gods and themselves?

5. How does the Greek outlook on the relationship of humankind to nature differ from that of other ancient Near Eastern peoples?

Answers

**CHAPTER 1
THE WORLD BEFORE
THE WEST**

Multiple—Choice

		Text Page
1.	C	2
2.	A	2
3.	D	3
4.	C	3-4
5.	B	6
6.	D	11-12
7.	C	12
8.	B	16
9.	A	18
10.	D	20

True/False

1.	T	3
2.	T	3
3.	T	9
4.	F	10
5.	F	13-15
6.	T	15
7.	T	17
8.	F	19
9.	F	20
10.	F	21

Completion

1.	Neolithic	3
2.	Sumerians	5
3.	Sargon	5
4.	Gilgamesh	8
5.	Akhnaton or Amenhotep IV	13-15
6.	Palestine	17
7.	Phoenicians	17
8.	one universal God	18
9.	Sekhmet	20
10.	Thales	21

◆ ◆ ◆ ◆ ◆ ◆

THE RISE OF GREEK CIVILIZATION

COMMENTARY

The story of the modem West is more closely associated with the rise of pre-Greek or Helladic civilization. Although clouded by some still unresolved questions about Cretan/Minoan civilization, it is clear that the influences on the Greek cultural tradition were Near Eastern, Mediterranean, and Asian. At Mycenae, in the northeastern comer of the Peloponnesus, the first mainland Helladic civilization flourished. Its strength was based on military exploits and on a widely deployed trade with other Near Eastern peoples. The influence of this palace/fortress centered civilization faded by 1200 B.C. with the Dorian invasion, but with the entire eastern end of the Mediterranean in disarray no new power emerged to fill the void. In this initially isolated environment the Greeks created the style of life and thought that has so marked the Western heritage.

This early period was dominated by the landed aristocrats, and the work of everyday life was carried on in large measure by free, but landless, laborers and some slaves. The Homeric legends reflected this society in which personal honor, physical courage, and the rights of property held high place. It was in the *polis* that the central themes of Greek history would develop. These independent communities, some of considerable size and urban complexity, were the symbols of Greek self-sufficiency and worldly satisfaction. It is clear that after the eighth century B.C. the *polis* played an increasingly important role in fostering the remarkable characteristics of the ancient Greeks. Although kingship existed, it was largely the aristocratic families who controlled the political, economic, and social life of the community. During this same period a remarkable advance in military technology appeared. The hoplite phalanx was a battlefield arrangement of heavily armed infantrymen. The key to success in battle lay in the discipline and training of the group (phalanx). Until the development of the legion formation of the Romans, the hoplite phalanx dominated the battles of the Greek world.

The expansion of Helladic civilization throughout the lands watered by the Mediterranean was simultaneous with the emergence of the *polis* and of the hoplite phalanx. In fact, each factor was interdependent on the other. Expansion brought the Greeks into contact with the large and small kingdoms of the ancient Near East. Greek colonies, established as independent, remained on excellent terms with the sponsoring city-state—a situation that stimulated trade and mutual dependency. The success of colonization during the eighth to the sixth century relieved considerable social and economic pressure from many *poleis* (plural of *polis*). The rise to wealth of some individuals outside of the traditional aristocracy caused new political and religious tensions leading to crisis proportions. This situation ushered in a new factor in Greek life-the tyrant, who, although from the ruling aristocracy, seized control of the state for himself and the faction that supported him. Often the tyrant had support of the hoplites and was thereby able to destroy the influence of the traditional leadership. The age of tyrants passed by the end of the sixth century B.C. Though repugnant to the idea of community and citizen responsibility, the tyrants had broken up the traditional hold over the *polis* of the wealthy landowners. Hence, their contributions to Greek life should not be scorned.

The primary example of city-state life and dynamics is found in an examination of the success of Sparta and Athens, which had risen to regional power in the sixth century B.C. The Spartan world was created by their successful conquest of the southern Peloponnesus in the Messenian wars. That position was maintained by the rigorous discipline of the Spartan citizens operating within a military caste system. The harsh upbringing of Spartan men and women assured their physical superiority over the less trained. Fully matured Spartan soldiers were in a class by themselves. The success of this system not only assured Sparta's place among the city-states but raised admiration from contemporary thinkers and moderns alike.

Initially the rise of Athens was triggered by increased commercial activity. Its location on the Attica peninsula jutting into the Mediterranean would keep Athenian economic growth steady for two centuries. Within that framework Athenian democracy was able to develop in a rational and cohesive way that ultimately benefited all classes of citizens there. The reforms of Solon early in the sixth century B.C. had a dual effect upon the class structure and the economic future of Athens. Before the democratic practices traditionally associated with Athenian life emerged, however, there was a period of tyrannical rule.

By the end of the sixth century B.C. some of the underlying forces of Greek life had been established. A polytheistic religion centered on a well-organized pantheon was a generally accepted function of the Greek way. Ethical considerations were a part not only of the religious tradition but also the poetic and philosophical. In this period the seeds of the Greek philosophical tradition that would flower in the next two centuries were sown, and these would set Western history on the path to the present.

The turning point of this phase of Greek history comes with the Persian Wars. The ancient Persian Empire (now Iran) under Cyrus, Cambyses, and Darius spread into Ionia toward the end of the sixth century B.C. The Athenians' support for the Ionian rebellion brought them to Persia's attention, and Athens was soon the object of a punitive expedition. What should have been a Persian success on the plain of Marathon on Attica's east coast was, surprisingly, a Greek victory. From this minor defeat Persia prepared to conquer all of Greece and a decade later smashed into southern Greece after the victory at Thermopylae Pass in 480 B.C. Before the Persians could consolidate their success, however, they were defeated at sea (Salamis) and on land (Plataea) and forced to withdraw. The Greek city-states were for a time saved from foreign intervention. It remained to be seen what would result from their triumph; but clearly the basis of the Greek (Hellenic) contribution to the Western heritage was established.

IDENTIFICATIONS

Identify each one of the following as used in the text. Refer to the text as necessary.

	Text Page
Minoan	24-25
Mycenaean	26-27
tholos tombs	26
Dorians	27-28
Agamemnon	29
arete	30
"an animal who lives in a *polis*"	30
hoplite	31
Magna Graecia	32
conquest of Messenia	34
helots	34
Draco	35
Solon	36
Areopagus	35
first Athenian tyranny	37-38
deme	38
Hesiod	39
Delphic Oracle	40
maenads	41
Sappho of Lesbos	41
Aristagoras	42
Xerxes	44
Greek League	44
Thermopylae Pass	44
Battle of Plataea	45

MAP EXERCISE A

Locate each of the following areas or places:

1. Dardenelles
2. Troy
3. Black Sea
4. Mycenae
5. Peloponnesus
6. Corinth
7. Pylos
8. Cnossus
9. Mt. Olympus
10. Sparta
11. Messenia
12. Attica
13. Athens
14. Salamis
15. Piraeus
16. Ionia
17. Delphi
18. Hellespont
19. Lesbos
20. Miletus
21. Marathon
22. Delos
23. Artemisium
24. Thermopylae Pass
25. Plataea
26. Macedonia
27. Thrace

CHAPTER 2
THE RISE OF GREEK CIVILIZATION

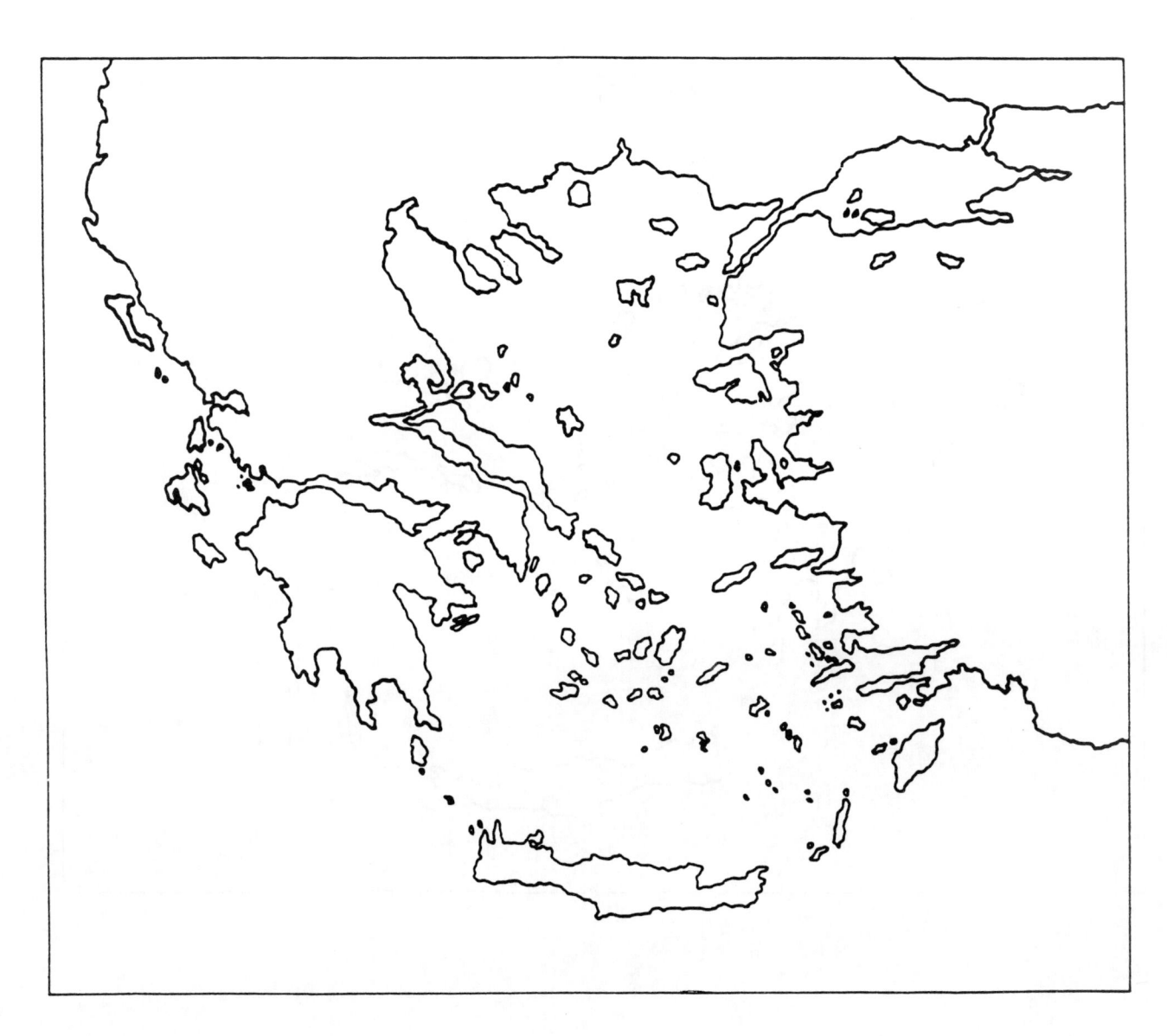

Map Exercise B

Mark the distance in kilometers and/or miles between each of the following cities/locations:

Athens	Lesbos	Piraeus
Corinth	Marathon	Salamis
Delos	Mt. Olympus	Sparta
Delphi	Mycenae	Thermopylae Pass

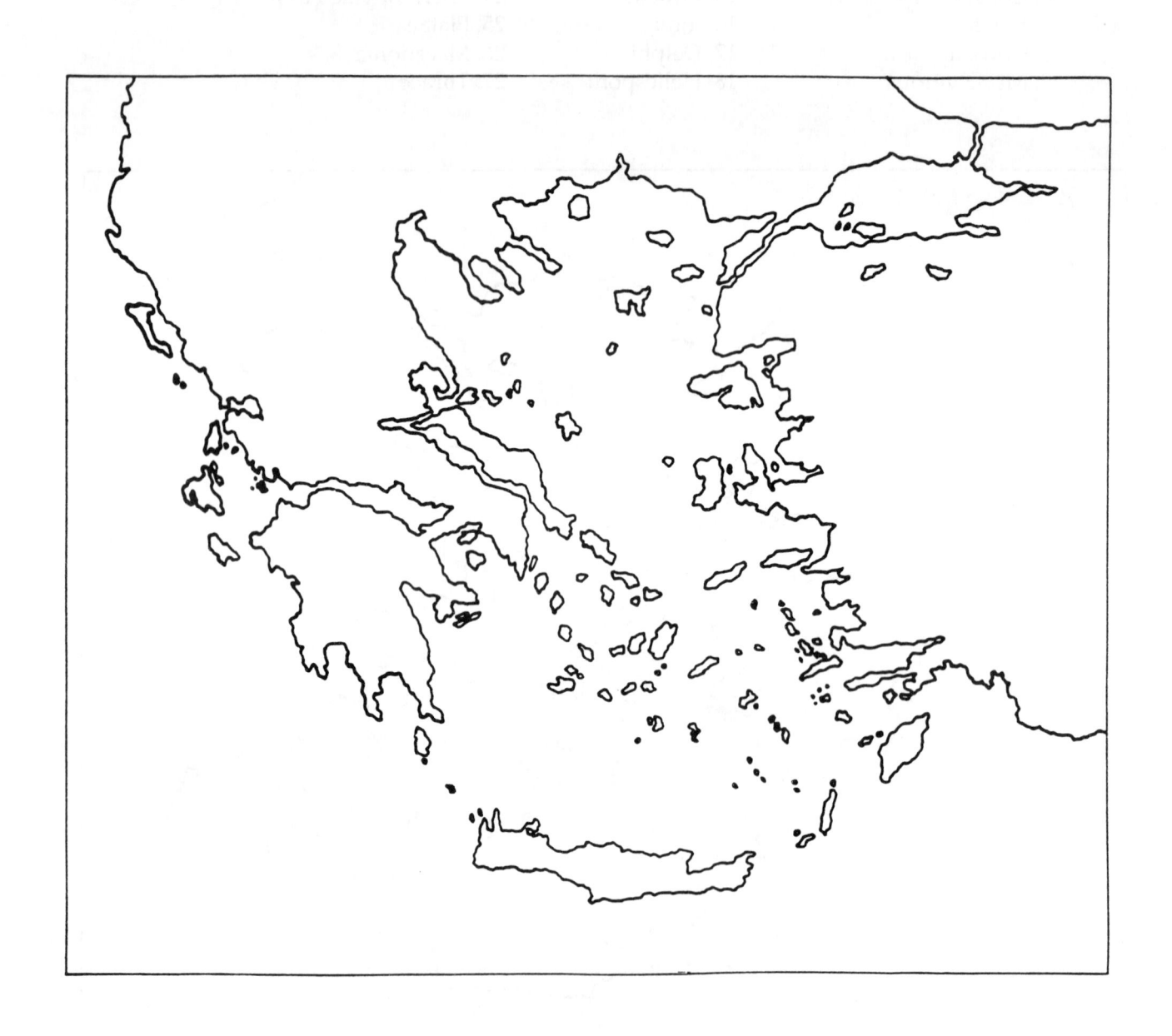

Short-Answer Exercises

Multiple-Choice

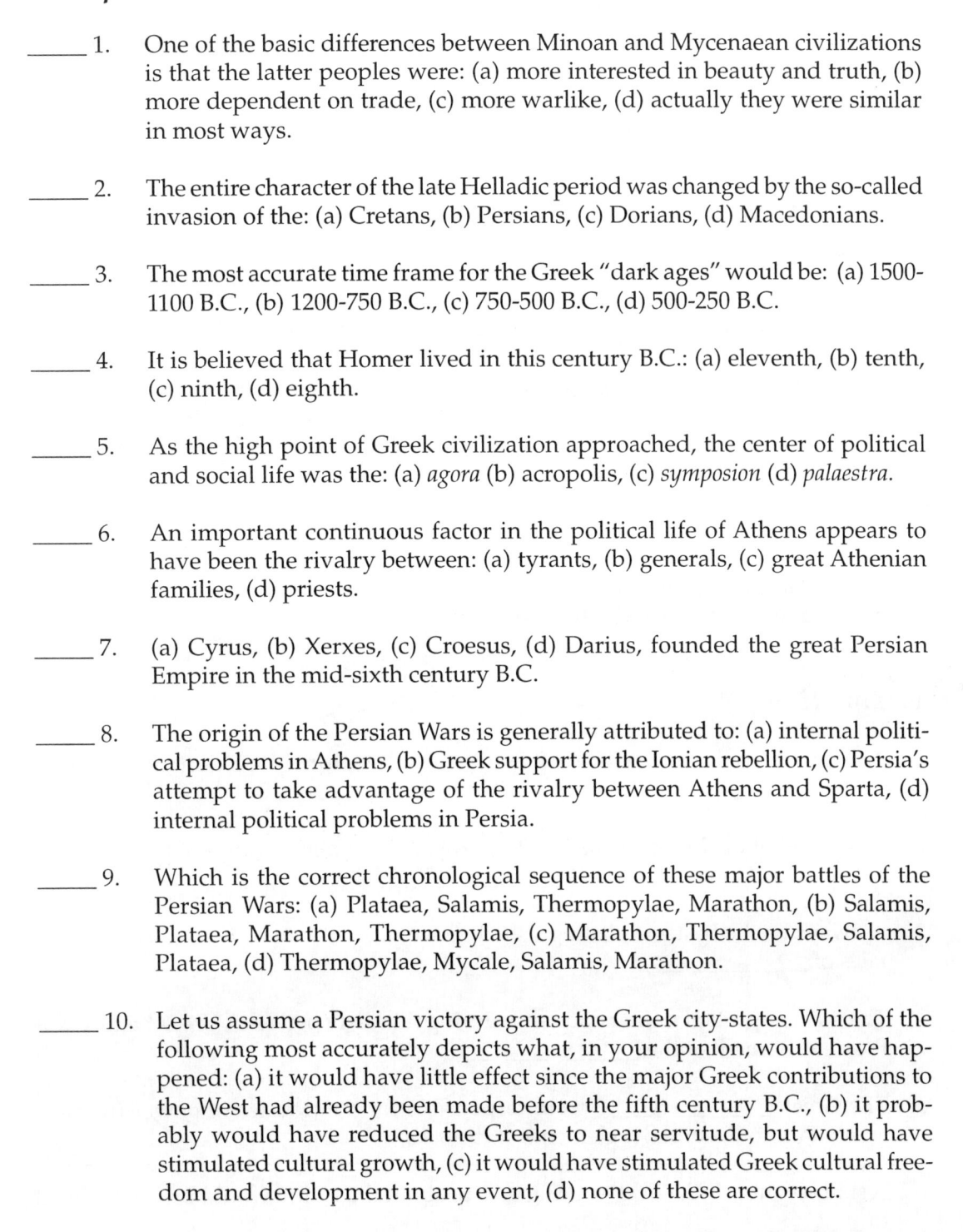

_____ 1. One of the basic differences between Minoan and Mycenaean civilizations is that the latter peoples were: (a) more interested in beauty and truth, (b) more dependent on trade, (c) more warlike, (d) actually they were similar in most ways.

_____ 2. The entire character of the late Helladic period was changed by the so-called invasion of the: (a) Cretans, (b) Persians, (c) Dorians, (d) Macedonians.

_____ 3. The most accurate time frame for the Greek "dark ages" would be: (a) 1500-1100 B.C., (b) 1200-750 B.C., (c) 750-500 B.C., (d) 500-250 B.C.

_____ 4. It is believed that Homer lived in this century B.C.: (a) eleventh, (b) tenth, (c) ninth, (d) eighth.

_____ 5. As the high point of Greek civilization approached, the center of political and social life was the: (a) *agora* (b) acropolis, (c) *symposion* (d) *palaestra*.

_____ 6. An important continuous factor in the political life of Athens appears to have been the rivalry between: (a) tyrants, (b) generals, (c) great Athenian families, (d) priests.

_____ 7. (a) Cyrus, (b) Xerxes, (c) Croesus, (d) Darius, founded the great Persian Empire in the mid-sixth century B.C.

_____ 8. The origin of the Persian Wars is generally attributed to: (a) internal political problems in Athens, (b) Greek support for the Ionian rebellion, (c) Persia's attempt to take advantage of the rivalry between Athens and Sparta, (d) internal political problems in Persia.

_____ 9. Which is the correct chronological sequence of these major battles of the Persian Wars: (a) Plataea, Salamis, Thermopylae, Marathon, (b) Salamis, Plataea, Marathon, Thermopylae, (c) Marathon, Thermopylae, Salamis, Plataea, (d) Thermopylae, Mycale, Salamis, Marathon.

_____ 10. Let us assume a Persian victory against the Greek city-states. Which of the following most accurately depicts what, in your opinion, would have happened: (a) it would have little effect since the major Greek contributions to the West had already been made before the fifth century B.C., (b) it probably would have reduced the Greeks to near servitude, but would have stimulated cultural growth, (c) it would have stimulated Greek cultural freedom and development in any event, (d) none of these are correct.

True-False

_____ 1. Sections of the palace at Cnossus are known to have been seven stories high.

_____ 2. *Tholos* tombs are interpreted as signs of the wealth and power of Mycenaean kings.

_____ 3. You are a man with "a dog's face and a deer's heart," is part of Achilles' address to the commander of the expedition against Troy.

_____ 4. A short spear was the normal weapon of a hoplite.

_____ 5. Homer wrote *Works and Days*.

_____ 6. Spartan boys normally began their military training at the age of seven.

_____ 7. The sole ruler of the Spartan city-state was called a tyrant.

_____ 8. Croesus of Lydia's alliance with Cyrus the Great was a key factor in starting the Persian Wars.

_____ 9. Miltiades was the Athenian commander at Marathon.

_____ 10. During the Persian Wars the Athenian Themistocles urged his city-state to imitate Sparta and rely on the army.

Completion

1. The most striking feature of Cretan civilization is evidenced by their _____.

2. The world of the Mycenaeans is better understood today because of the discovery at Cnossus of tablets known as _____.

3. "Always be the best and distinguished above others," can be associated with the tales of _____.

4. The most important military advance during this early period of Greek history was the development of the _____.

5. The Greek _____ were responsible for the transfer of power from the aristocracy to the broader elements of the *polis*.

6. A sixth-century B.C. Greek seeking advice about the future would probably travel to _____.

7. _____ was the Greek god of excessive pleasures.

8. Theognis of Megara actually divided people into honorable _____ and base _____.

9. In the battle of Thermopylae Pass, the city-state of _____ sacrificed a king and 300 soldiers.

10. By the year _____ B.C. the Persian threat to Greece appeared to have passed.

For Further Consideration

1. Modern scholars have suggested several theories to explain the apparent destruction of Mycenaean civilization. Describe and discuss several of these theories.

2. Discuss the idea of the "hero" in Greek literature and thought.

3. What was the Greek view of the concept of citizenship? How is this concept similar to and how is it different from that of the Egyptians and Mesopotamians, and from today's concept?

4. How did the battle of Marathon affect the Athenians? How did it effect the Persians? From a military point of view, how are the Greek city-states with all of their rivalries able to defeat the great empire of Persia?

5. Compare and contrast the world of early Greek civilization (1500-500 B.C.) with the early development of the civilizations in Mesopotamia and Egypt.

Answers

Multiple-Choice

		Text Page
1.	C	26
2.	C	27-28
3.	B	28/25
4.	D	29
5.	A	31
6.	C	35/*passim*
7.	A	41
8.	B	42
9.	C	44-45
10.	D	*passim*

True-False

1.	F	24-25
2.	T	26
3.	T	29
4.	F	31
5.	T	34
6.	F	34
7.	F	39
8.	F	41
9.	T	44
10.	F	44

Completion

1.	palaces	24
2.	Linear B	25
3.	Homer	30
4.	hoplite phalanx	31
5.	tyrants	33
6.	Delphi	40
7.	Dionysus	41
8.	noble/commoners	41
9.	Sparta	44
10.	479 B.C.	45

◆ ◆ ◆ ◆ ◆ ◆ ◆

Chapter 3

CLASSICAL AND HELLENISTIC GREECE

COMMENTARY

The end of the Persian threat effectively split the reek city-states into two groupings: the Spartan dominated Peloponnesian League and the Delian League controlled by the Athenians. The increasing prestige and influence of Athens over the other poleis within the League was becoming evident, as a uniquely democratic governmental system was developing there. While Athenians enjoyed a freer society in this period, most persons and virtually all women were denied participation in the life of the polis. Slavery existed within the most democratic society of this era. And while representing a substantial portion (note the debate over the actual numbers involved on p. 90) of the population, it should be noted, how different the characteristics of Athenian slavery were from that found in pre-Civil War America.

Though the origins of the Great Peloponnesian War were not directly connected with Athens and Sparta, these two states were drawn into the contest by lesser forces beyond their control. In 431 B.C. Sparta, siding with Corinth, invaded Attica. The war remained a seesaw affair for decades. Though interspersed with occasional truce periods, peace remained elusive and in the end, the Athenians, having suffered defeats in Sicily and at the naval disaster at Aegospotami, surrendered in 404 B.C. Sparta in victory quickly replaced Athens as the imperialist power though her history and government made her ill-suited to the role. The Greek troubles continued as Persian interventions, a resurgence of Athens, and the challenges of Thebes underscored the continued erosion of Spartan power. By the middle of the fourth century B.C., after 200 years of warfare and glory, the Greek *poleis* returned to the instability of an earlier era.

Although the struggles of the fifth and fourth centuries B.C. create an aggressive and warlike image of classical Greece, it is truly the culture of those centuries that best reflects the inner dynamics and tensions of the era. The early victory over the great empire of Persia had acted as a catalyst to the cultural expressions found in the *poleis*. The famous Greek tragedies which appeared in this era were reflective of the inner struggles and basic themes of Greek life. It is in philosophy, however, that the Greek contribution surpasses the influence not only of other Greek works but reaches through two thousand years of Western history to the present day. The philosophical teachings of these ancient Greeks became the keystone of the edifice of civilization. The teachings of the Sophists brought many of the accepted traditions of the *polis* into open discussion and acted as the stimuli for the responses of Socrates in the fifth century B.C. and the renowned Plato and Aristotle in the fourth century B.C. Whereas the Sophists attempted to resolve immediate and pragmatic concerns, ancient Greek historians sought to explain the inner motivations of human action within the political arena. Herodotus and Thucydides more than just chronicled the events they witnessed in the fifth century B.C.; they offered accurate pictures of what happened and suggested the relationship of these events to the wider concerns of humankind.

By the opening of the fourth century B.C., it was clear that the long warfare between Athens and Sparta had caused irreversible damage to the fabric of Greek life. Internal strife and economic disorder followed in the wake of those wars. Cultural expressions were revised and became somewhat reflective of this period of disillusionment.

The death of Socrates in 399 B.C. has remained for Western peoples a symbolic martyrdom because of his professed individualism and uncompromising demand for intellectual truth. The emphasis on reason, not relative but absolute, put him a cut above his fellow sophists. Socrates remains one of the great tragic figures of all time. The school of cynicism that followed in the wake of Socrates' teachings put an even greater emphasis, at times exaggerated, on the distant future than on the immediate past. As citizens of the world, the cynics were forerunners of the thinkers of the Hellenistic era.

A more conclusive response to the difficulties of the time, with the corresponding weakening of the *poleis*, comes from Plato and Aristotle. Their contribution to the Western philosophical tradition can never be overstated. Plato's philosophy aimed not only at the redemption of the *polis* in the fourth century B.C. but at the philosophical salvation of humankind through a systematic and comprehensive inquiry into the nature of truth. As Plato's pupil, Aristotle reached beyond the teachings of his mentor to collect and assemble many areas of humanistic and scientific knowledge. The subjects treated in the Lyceum ranged across the scientific and philosophical spectrum. The great thinkers of this age, however, were concerned not only with the metaphysical and epistemological problems of their philosophy, but also with a patriotic concern for the life of the *polis* of classical Greece, a concern that came too late.

By the middle of the fourth century B.C. the Greek city-states were ripe for external conquest. They did not have to wait long. Macedonia, long on the fringes of Greek civilization, yet with a similar culture, heritage, and people, bade for supremacy at this time. A young king, Philip II, entered Macedonia into the unsettled politics of the *poleis*. As his son Alexander would eventually demonstrate, the Macedonians were capable warriors and, at times, shrewd diplomats. A carrot-and-stick policy, backed by an unusually large army, brought Macedonia into control of the Greek city-states. By 338 B.C. Philip was master of Greece and already contemplating an assault upon Greece's traditional rival—the Persian Empire. A recent archaeological discovery bears further witness to Philip's greatness. His death temporarily stalled the invasion, but his son Alexander, his successor at age twenty, continued with the preparations. The campaign against Persia began in 334 B.C., and Alexander's forces, though short-supplied, carried the important battle at the Granicus River. As they marched inland, success followed upon success. The young king's tactical skill and personal bravery brought the speedy conquest of Egypt and a continuation of the campaign into east Asia. After the treacherous elimination of the king of Persia by his own supporters, the Persians remained unable to stem the Macedonians and their allies in the advance. Alexander's conquest took him to northern India, and from there his tired army returned to Babylon in 324 B.C. Alexander died there the following year. It remained to be seen if the vast empire so quickly acquired could be held together by his successors. Within a century of Alexander's death the areas he had conquered would be open to new conquests from the growing republic of Rome in the western Mediterranean. Alexander's military campaigns are often viewed as his single contribution to Western history, but they are, in fact, eclipsed by the contributions of the era his victories ushered in—a world of Greeklike culture imbued with a universal spirit—in short, the Hellenistic world.

The Hellenistic world was the symbol of a cultural shift that soon engulfed the eastern end of the Mediterranean. Gone was the intellectual self-assurance of the classical era, that era so dominated by the spirit of the *polis*. It was replaced by an outlook disposed to accept and deal with the position of man in this universe. Life became less speculative, philosophy more compromising, and scientific achievement, though not in all fields, widespread. Acceptance of life, fate, became a theme of the Epicureans and the Stoics. Scientists and humanists alike were able to make substantial contributions to knowledge through their work at the schools and libraries established at Alexandria. The arts reflected this changing mood. Mathematics and physics were studied with enthusiasm, and the achievements in these fields laid the foundation of much of Western thought almost to modem times.

The Hellenistic spirit, in the spreading of the Greek cultural tradition and despite the uncertainties of the age, left a lasting imprint on the Western heritage.

IDENTIFICATIONS

Identify each one of the following as used in the text. Refer to the text as necessary.

	Text Page
Cimon	48-49
Pericles	49-52
Thirty Years' Peace	51
epikleros	53
hektemoroi	54
Alcibiades	56
Lysander	57
Sophists	61
Cynics	64
Academy	64
episteme	65
Lyceum	65
Peripatetics	65
Philip II	67
Isocrates	67
Battle of Chaeronea	68
Darius III	68-71
Granicus River	68
Gaugamela	71
Bessus	71
Alexander Eschate	71
Princess Roxane	71-72
Epicurus	73
ataraxia	74
Zeno	74
"the virtuous life"	74

Map Exercise A

Locate each of these modern states on the map of the world according to Eratosthenes:

1. Spain
2. Italy
3. England/Scotland
4. Ireland
5. France
6. Germany
7. Switzerland
8. Russia
9. Egypt
10. Libya
11. India
12. Israel
13. Iran
14. China

Map Exercise B

Utilizing this copy of the map appearing on page 70 of the text, list below all of the contemporary nations that Alexander The Great passed through.

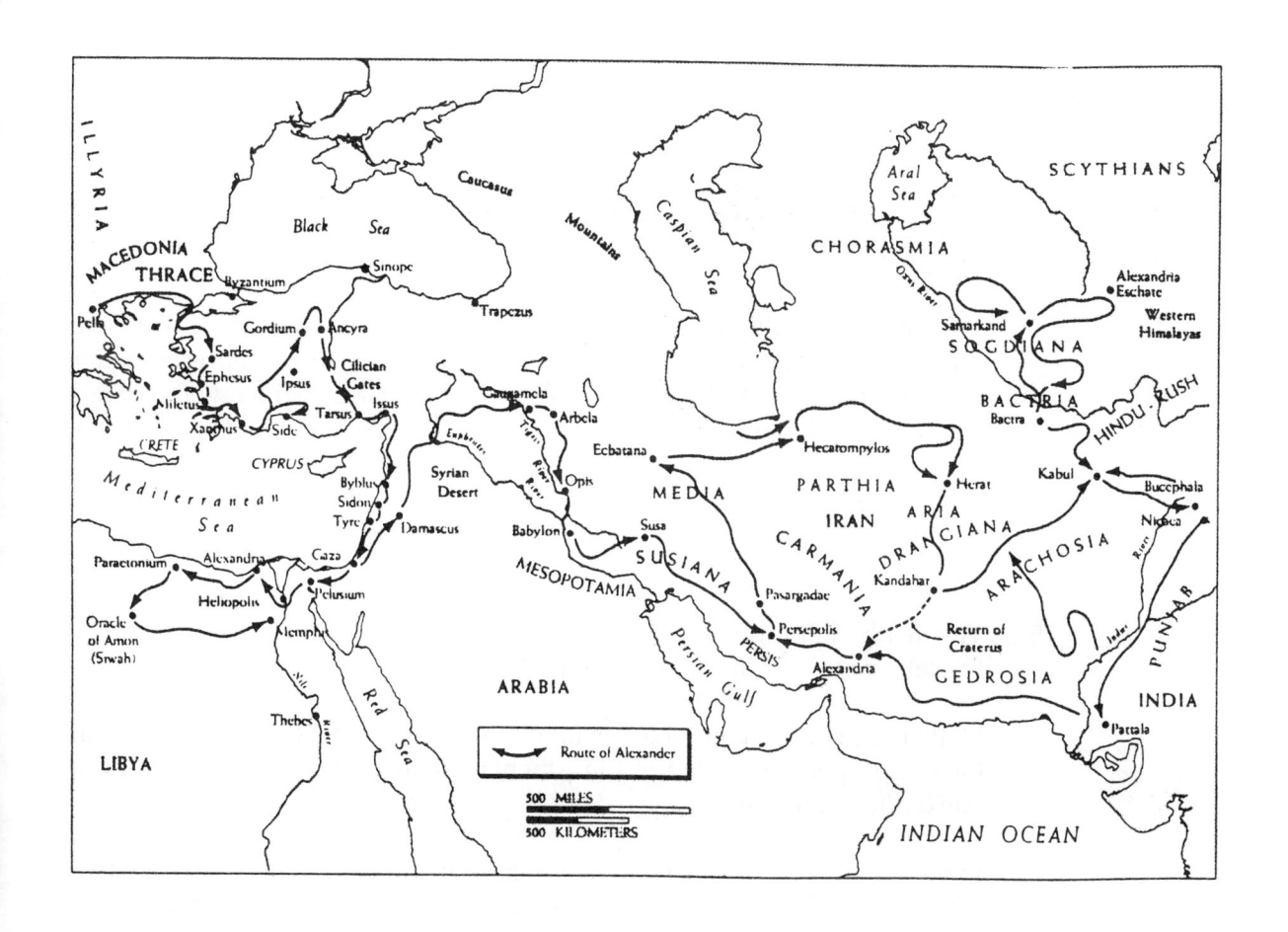

Short-Answer Exercises

Multiple-Choice

_____ 1. With the end of the Persian threat the Greek world divided into spheres of influence dominated by: (a) Thebes and Thrace, (b) Athens and Sparta, (c) Sparta and Corinth, (d) Athens and Macedonia.

_____ 2. The almost continuous success of Pericles as an elected leader of Athens can be attributed primarily to: (a) his willingness to use corruption for his own advancement (b) his subtle use of police power against all opposition, (c) his skill as a general and politician, (d) his open contempt toward philosophers.

_____ 3. The founding of the Second Athenian Confederation in 378 B.C.: (a) led to a repeat of the abuses associated with the Delian League, (b) represented far less power than the Delian League, (c) soon faced Athens with revolts against her rule, (d) all of these.

_____ 4. The increased Macedonian wealth of the fourth century B.C. derived from: (a) piracy, (b) internal taxation, (c) gold and silver mines, (d) corrupt politicians.

_____ 5. The death of Philip II of Macedonia was: (a) clearly murder, (b) suspicious, (c) definitely natural, (d) none of these.

_____ 6. Hellenistic culture tended to be: (a) mainly a rural one, (b) concentrated in Greece proper, (c) limited to the Athenian state, (d) rooted in the cities of Alexander's empire.

_____ 7. In the philosophy of Stoicism the principle aim of man is: (a) a virtuous life, (b) a pleasurable life, (c) a life of religious devotion, (d) none of these.

_____ 8. The idea of a grid pattern for ancient Greek cities is associated with: (a) Epicurus of Athens, (b) Heraclides of Pontus, (c) Hippodamus of Miletus, (d) Eratosthenes of Cyrene.

_____ 9. The basis of modern geometry is based on a work written by: (a) Euclid, (b) Archimedes, (c) Ptolemy, (d) Copernicus.

_____ 10. A clearly recognizable sun centered (heliocentric) view of the universe is associated with: (a) Aristotle, (b) Ptolemy of Alexandria, (c) Euclid, (d) Aristarchus of Samos.

True/False

_____ 1. Though Athens gained a strategic advantage, the alliance with Megara brought on the First Peloponnesian War.

_____ 2. The popular courts of Athens to which any citizen could appeal contained between 51 and 1501 jurors.

_____ 3. While Athenian women had no choice of husbands, they retained control of their dowry throughout the marriage.

_____ 4. For Empedocles of Acragas the four basic elements were: fire, earth, love, and strife.

_____ 5. The leading playwright of the so-called New Comedy of the late fourth century B.C. was Menander.

_____ 6. When compared to Socrates and Plato, Aristotle actually had the longest life span.

_____ 7. Most of our knowledge today of Aristotle's work is the product of what are believed to be his student's lecture notes.

_____ 8. The longer pike of thirteen feet utilized by the Macedonians was called a companion.

_____ 9. Ptolemy I, Seleucus I, and Antigonus I are the names of the Macedonian generals that assumed power over major areas of what had been Alexander's empire.

_____ 10. Hellenistic contributions to our knowledge of geography can be said to originate in the works of Euclid.

Completion

1. The approximate distance between the city-states of Athens and Sparta was _____ kilometers.

2. The defeat of the Athenian navy at _____ in 405 B.C. was practically the last straw in Athens' defeat in the Great Peloponnesian War.

3. In the early 4th century B.C. the city-state of _____ controlled Boeotia and exercised a wide influence in Greece after the Great Peloponnesian War.

4. _____ wrote the history of the Great Peloponnesian War.

5. The humility and disdain for worldly things exemplified by Socrates was carried to extremes by _____ and the _____.

6. One of the reasons for the success of the Macedonian army was an innovative change in the traditional Greek _____.

7. _____ of Athens believed that a Greek supported Macedonian invasion of Persia would yield beneficial economic and political results.

8. The conquest of Persia by the Macedonians essentially ended Alexander's, later the Great, _____ problems.

9. Epicurean philosophy attempted to eliminate one's fear of _____.

10. Stoics believed that human fulfillment was the result of living in harmony with _____.

FOR FURTHER CONSIDERATION

1. Discuss in detail the causes and overall effects of the Peloponnesian Wars.

2. Herodotus and Thucydides are considered founders of the modem concept of history. What difficulties would they have encountered in preparing their histories as compared to modem scholars and students today?

3. From your understanding of the activities and achievements of Alexander of Macedon, does he deserve the title of "great"? Explain your answer fully.

4. How does Hellenistic philosophy as expressed through the teachings of the Stoics and Epicureans differ from that of classical Greece?

5. Describe the overall characteristics of the Hellenistic world's life-style and outlook. What were the main contributions to the West of the Hellenistic age?

Answers

Multiple-Choice

		Text Page
1.	B	48
2.	C	52
3.	D	58
4.	C	67
5.	A	68
6.	D	73
7.	A	74
8.	C	75
9.	A	76
10.	A	76

True/False

1.	T	50
2.	T	52
3.	F	53
4.	F	61
5.	T	62-63
6.	F	63-65
7.	F	65
8.	F	67
9.	T	72
10.	F	76

Completion

1.	175	49
2.	Aegospotami	56
3.	Thebes	58
4.	Thucydides	62
5.	Diogenes/Cynics	64
6.	phalanx	67
7.	Isocrates	67-68
8.	financial	71
9.	death	73
10.	nature	74

◆ ◆ ◆ ◆ ◆ ◆ ◆

ROME: FROM REPUBLIC TO EMPIRE

COMMENTARY

From the end of the Neolithic period until the emergence of the Roman Republic, the Italian Peninsula was largely dominated by the Etruscans. Early Roman government reflected both the Etruscan tradition and the agrarian nature of Roman society. The elected king had broad imperial powers but other sectors of government, the Senate and the Assembly, had specific roles. In time it was the Senate, as the republic became powerful in the Mediterranean world, that would dominate Roman political, economic, and social life. The Roman family was the center of that life. The positions of family members were traditionally clear. Through all of Roman life and history the struggle between the patricians and plebeians remained an important factor in the development of constitutional Rome after 509 B.C.

Initially the key to Rome's success lay in the varied, yet capable, way they handled their opponents. They fought invaders from the north as well as restless neighbors and thereby maintained their position in central Italy. By the time of Carthage's challenge in the mid-third century, the Roman Republic's position in Mediterranean affairs had been acknowledged. The struggle with Carthage, lasting more than a century, became a dominant feature of Roman life; and remained a central fact of Roman history. Rome's success, control of new lands and peoples, brought new problems to the republic, which continued to grow at the expense of eastern Mediterranean powers. Macedonia, Greece, Egypt, and other Eastern kingdoms would soon experience the competition of Rome. Victory followed victory, bringing increased prestige and wealth to the political leaders and generals of Rome and direct benefits to most classes of Roman citizens. In time, fundamental changes of attitude and policies toward conquered lands and peoples emerged with Rome's success. An early ambivalence toward the *Greek poleis* soon gave way to increasing control over them. Continued fortune and expansion in Spain and the western Mediterranean led to the salting of Carthage in 146 B.C., a symbol of Roman power and future policy. Old Roman traditions and outlooks were transformed by their association with Hellenistic Greeks. Although Roman attitudes varied toward the Greeks and their culture, the Romans did not refute the intellectual achievements of these contemporaries.

It was increasingly clear by the end of the second century B.C. that a principally agrarian people by hard work, tenacity, luck, and sacrifice had come to rule the shores of the Mediterranean Sea. The time had come for Rome to face the fact that it had become an empire, and the early attempts at reform, particularly those associated with the Gracchi brothers, should be viewed as the initial stages of the transformation from a republic to an empire.

At first, Tiberius, and later his brother Gaius, by gaining popular support, were able to propose land reform legislation that threatened the existing order. Their violent deaths ushered in a new era of political maneuvering. As foreign threats continued in northern Africa and southern Gaul the senate elected C. Marius to the consulship. This capable soldier soon led Rome's legions to victory, secured several more consular terms, and began a sweeping reform of the military. These apparent innovations in the army, which emphasized a new professional character, would ultimately hurt the republic and the empire in the future. Though Marius was called on again by the Senate, he was never accorded the honors he expected. Instead another successful soldier, C. Sulla, followed in his footsteps, and when Marius attempted to return, civil war ensued. In the battles that followed, Sulla's forces won out, and he ruthlessly punished his opponents' supporters. Roman politics was a bloody business indeed. The effect of Sulla's use of the military to grab power far outweighed the constitutional reforms he initiated.

The end of the republic was in sight as extraordinary senatorial actions continued to erode the basic principles of the Roman constitutional system. Ambitious generals and self-serving tribunes underscored the assault upon Roman tradition begun in the days of the Gracchi. The jealous rivalries between Pompey and Crassus set the stage for the political intrigues of the 60s B.C. The alignment of Crassus with the young Julius Caesar would soon pay dividends for both of them. Cicero's elimination of the Catiline conspiracy ended a threat from yet another quarter. The formation of the First Triumvirate in 60 B.C., which brought three competitors into an informal political alliance, was a further blow to the stability of the republic. For his participation in the Triumvirate, Caesar was given his wish for a military command. For almost ten years Caesar would lead Roman armies against the Gauls. The capable legions under his command brought Gaul under control by 56 B.C. However, additional consolidation was necessary. His maturing military ability and leadership would carry forward the task, bringing him considerable wealth and prestige. His new position as conqueror of Gaul made him an equal within the Triumvirate.

After 50 B.C. he was ready to return to Rome. The death of Crassus in the East a few years earlier made it increasingly probable that a new civil war, pitting Caesar against Pompey, would not be long in waiting. An attempted compromise between them collapsed in 49 B.C. and Caesar's legions were ordered across the Rubicon. For almost two years Caesar pursued Pompey throughout the republic, his veteran legions performing with great skill and loyalty. His lenient policies toward his enemy's followers increased his chance of success and his popularity. As Caesar edged closer to victory, Pompey escaped to Egypt, there to lose his head at the hands of an incapable monarch. Caesar soon arrived in Egypt and drank in the pleasures of antiquity, including those of Cleopatra. By 45 B.C. he was master of Rome. Caesar's reform program was cut short by his murder the following year. That program increased benefits to the poor, extended Roman citizenship to greater numbers of non-Romans, reduced the influence of the Senate, carried out sweeping financial reforms, and cleared up a basic problem in the Roman calendar. Despite these changes, his position within the republic was uncertain. Should he remain as dictator or go the additional and somewhat radical step of establishing a monarchy? The fear of the latter caused a senatorial conspiracy to form and in 44 B.C. this group assassinated him. The anticipated popularity of the conspirators never materialized. They were not seen as saviors of the republic but rather as evil adventurers. They were quickly declared outlaws by Mark Antony and by Caesar's heir Octavian. Antony, Octavian, and Lepidus formed the Second Triumvirate of Roman history in order to rule with wide authority and to facilitate the pursuit of the assassins. The men of the Second Triumvirate, like those of the first, soon became involved in civil war. By 31 B.C., after years of struggle between Mark Antony in the East at Alexandria and Octavian in the West at Rome, the issue of supremacy within the Roman state was finally settled at the important naval battle at Actium off the western coast of Greece. At age 32, Octavian had achieved a unified rule over the Roman ship of state. After 100 years of political violence and civil war it appeared that a stabilizing leader had taken the helm. The peace of imperial Rome would follow; the republic was finished.

IDENTIFICATIONS

Identify each one of the following as used in the text. Refer to the text as necessary.

	Text Page
Etruscans	80-81
imperium	81
curiate assembly	81
clientage	82
consuls	83
censor	84
centuriate assembly	84
nobiles	85
Mamertines	88
Barca family of Carthage	89-90
Cato	91
Livius Andronicus	92
grammaticus	93
latifundia	96
populares and *optimates*	98-99
Gaius Gracchus	99
C. Marius	99-100
L. C. Sulla	100-101
Catiline plot	102
First Triumvirate	102
Second Triumvirate	103-104
Battle of Actium	104

MAP EXERCISE A

Locate/outline each of the following on the accompanying map:

1. land of the Etruscans
2. city of Rome
3. Tiber valley
4. Cisalpine Gaul
5. city of Messana
6. Hannibal's march
7. city of Carthage
8. Palestine
9. Macedonia
10. Po Valley
11. city of Brundisium
12. Numidia
13. Egypt
14. Parthia
15. Mauretania
16. Munda
17. Actium
18. Roman world at the accession of Octavian

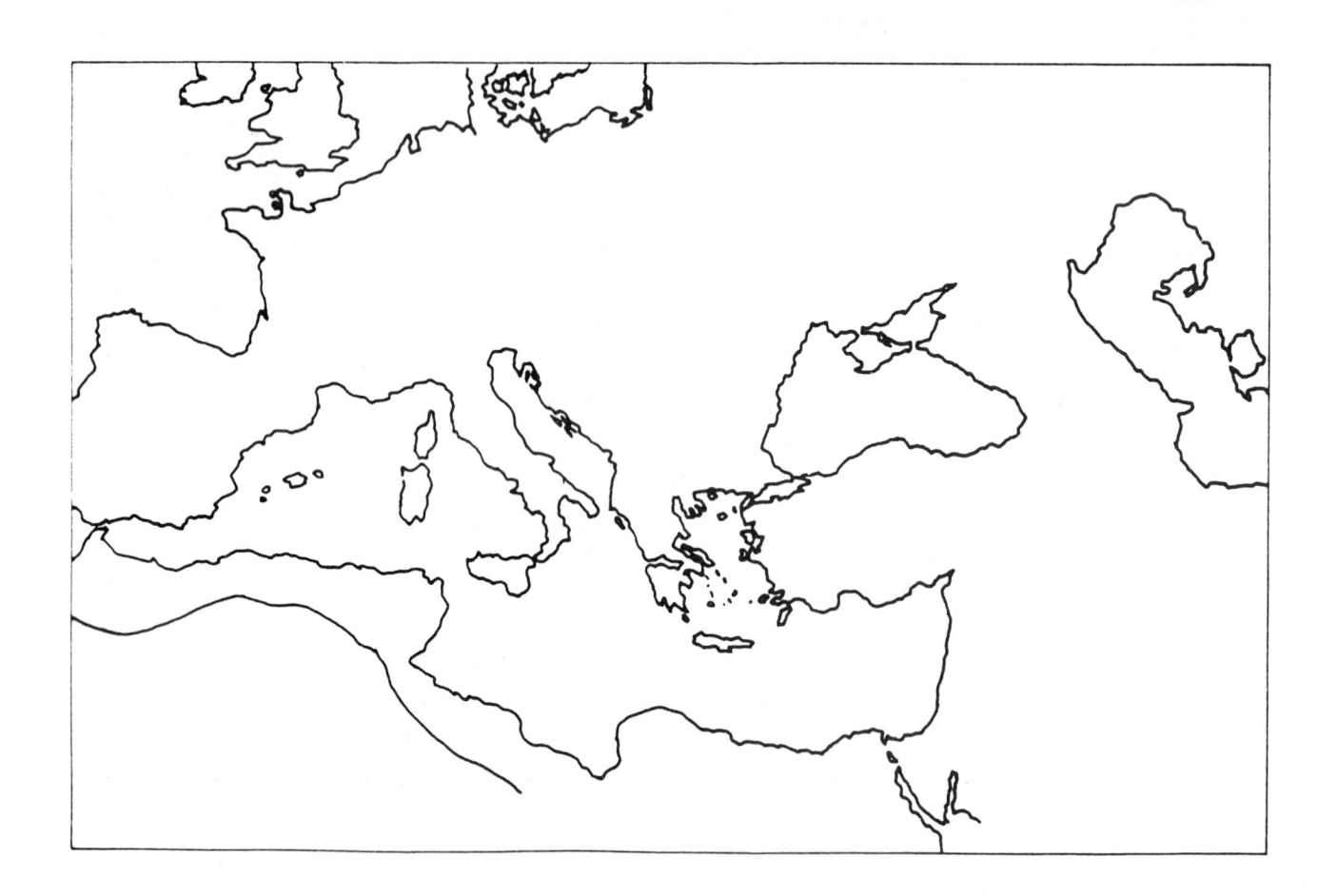

Map Exercise B

Locate each of the following bodies of water:

1. Adriatic Sea
2. Aegean Sea
3. Black Sea
4. Caspian Sea
5. Gulf of Corinth
6. "Our Sea"
7. Strait of Messina
8. Red Sea
9. Tyrrhenian Sea

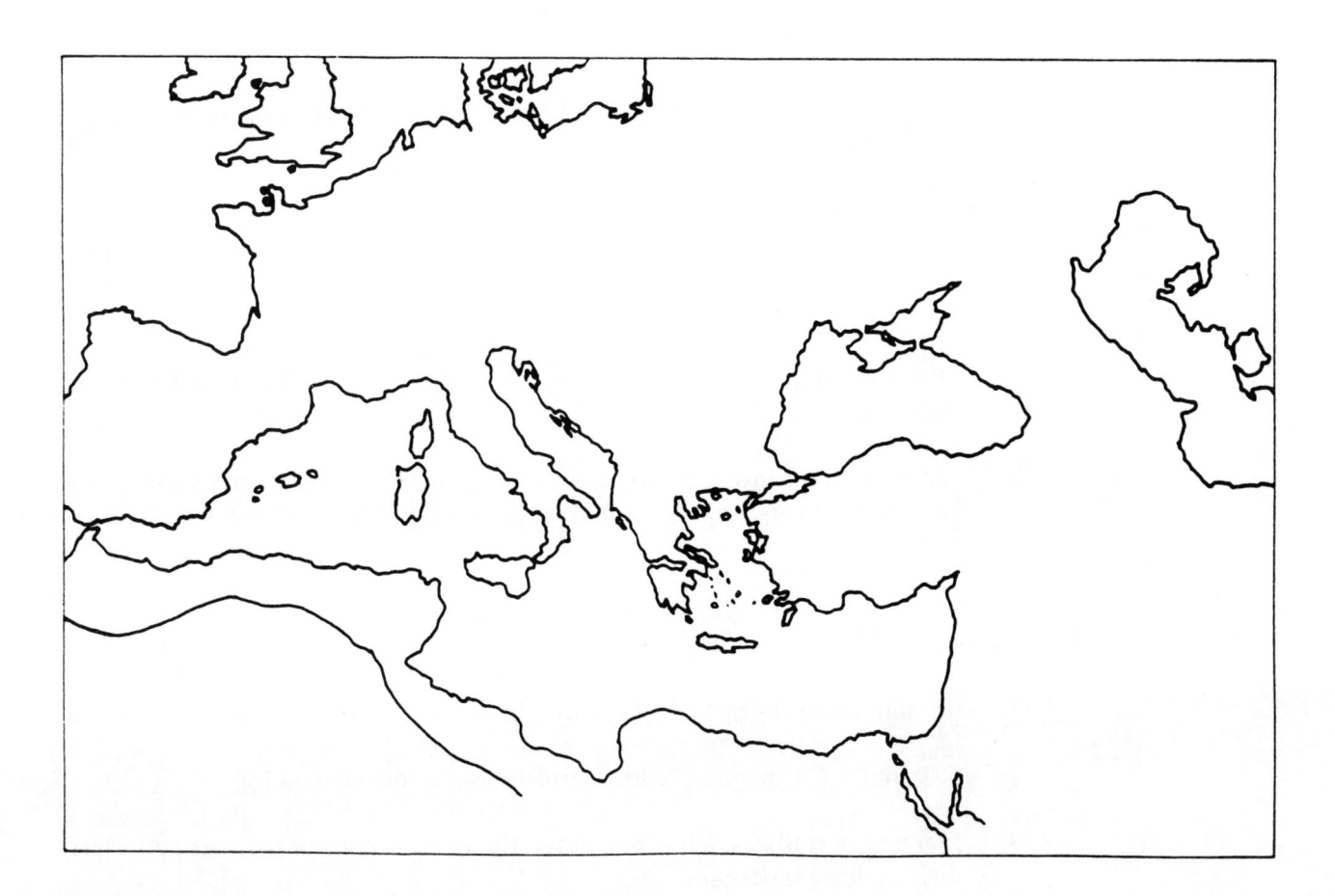

Short-Answer Exercises

Multiple-Choice

1. At the start of the Roman Republic, the patricians guarded their status by: (a) forbidding marriage with plebeians, (b) maintaining the slave-like status of the plebeians, (c) keeping a close eye on their political opponents, (d) using the practice of clientage to their advantage.

2. Ultimately the Roman Republic came to be dominated by: (a) the consuls, (h) the senatorial aristocracy, (c) the army, (d) the tribunes of the people.

_A̶ D_ 3. The worst military defeat in Roman history occurred during the wars with Carthage at: (a) the Ebro, River, (b) the Ticinus River, (c) Zama, (d) Cannae.

_D_ 4. The Roman general Publius Cornelius Scipio (Africanus) was successful in the Second Punic War because: (a) he was a talented military leader, (b) he conquered Spain thereby stemming reinforcements to Hannibal, (c) he was able to attack Carthage while Hannibal was still in Italy, (d) all of these are correct.

_D_ 5. Roman education was designed to make young boys: (a) patriotic and law-abiding, (b) moral and pious, (c) respectful of Roman tradition, (d) all of these.

_D̶ C_ 6. Near the end of the Roman Republic slaves accounted for (a) 20%, (b) 30%, (c) 40%, (d) 50% of the population of Italy.

_____ 7. Central to the reform program of the Gracchi brothers was: (a) redistribution of land, (b) freeing of slaves, (c) increased authority for tribunes, (d) reduction of senatorial power.

_____ 8. The first Triumvirate was composed of: (a) Caesar, Cicero, Pompey, (b) Crassus, Pompey, Caesar, (c) Brutus, Caesar, Catiline, (d) Cato, Cicero, Caesar.

_____ 9. Of approximately 900 Senators, about: (a) 6, (b) 36, (c) 60, (d) 600, were involved in the plot to murder Julius Caesar.

_____ 10. The Second Triumvirate was composed of: (a) Pompey, Brutus, Cassius, (b) Octavian, Brutus, Lepidus, (c) Mark Antony, Agrippa, Maecenas, (d) Mark Antony, Octavian, Lepidus.

True-False

_____ 1. Roman political practices show the clearest evidence of Etruscan influence.

_____ 2. Originally, Carthage in North Africa was a Phoenician colony.

_____ 3. Mercenary soldiers, who considered themselves sons of the war god Mars, were called Martians.

_____ 4. As the Romans increased their role in the Mediterranean world it became clear to them that military campaigns could be profitable.

_____ 5. The murder of Tiberius Gracchus and his followers is an important watershed of the Republic because it was the first politically motivated bloodshed within the state.

_____ 6. By Marius's consulship impoverished volunteers for the Roman legions viewed enlistment as an opportunity to obtain land and other rewards in exchange for their service.

_____ 7. The initial claim of M. L. Crassus to prominence in Rome stemmed from his defeat of Mithridates.

_____ 8. The First Triumvirate was formed by J. Caesar, C. Pompey, and A. Brescia.

_____ 9. Caesar's military triumphs in Gaul gave him the fame and power needed to advance his political ambitions.

_____ 10. Among his many internal reforms, Caesar substantially increased the number of Roman senators.

Completion

1. The center of Roman life was the _____.

2. Winning a battle, but suffering heavy casualties, is referred to as a _____.

3. Carthage's most talented general was _____.

4. A Greek slave accompanying a young Roman boy to school was called a _____.

5. The Roman slave system had the effect of changing the _____ composition of their people.

6. Success in the Jugurthine War in Numidia helped the political career of _____.

7. _____ rose to political power in the 70's B.C. commanding one of the special units which operated without constitutional restrictions.

8. In large measure, connections through marriage and in-laws helped the initial political career of _____.

9. The idea of creating a "harmony of orders" is associated with the Roman politician _____.

10. _____ and _____ are among the better known names of Caesar's murderers.

FOR FURTHER CONSIDERATION

1. Describe the Roman Republic's policies toward conquered peoples. Imagine yourself as a Roman senator of this era. What suggestions would you make or endorse with regard to conquered enemies?

2. What were the causes and historical significance of Rome's wars against Carthage?

3. Describe the style of education available in the early Roman Republic? In your opinion, why was the emphasis on young men? Briefly comment on what you see were the key differences between Roman education of young men and young women?

4. Compare and contrast the origins of the First Triumvirate with the Second Triumvirate. How did each relate to the Roman constitution?

5. In your opinion, was Julius Caesar's threat to the Senate and the political foundations of the Roman Republic real or imagined? Explain your answer fully.

ANSWERS

Multiple-Choice

		Text Page
1.	A	82
2.	B	85
3.	D	90
4.	D	90
5.	D	92
6.	C	96
7.	A	98
8.	B	102
9.	C	103
10.	D	103

True-False

1.	F	81
2.	T	87
3.	F	88
4.	T	91
5.	T	98
6.	T	100
7.	F	101
8.	F	102
9.	T	103
10.	T	103

Completion

1.	family	82
2.	Pyrrhic victory	87
3.	Hannibal Barca	90
4.	*paedagogus*	93
5.	ethnic	96
6.	C. Marius	100
7.	Pompey	101
8.	G. Julius Caesar	102
9.	Cicero	102
10.	Gaius Cassius Longinus/ Marcus Junius Brutus	103

◆ ◆ ◆ ◆ ◆ ◆

Chapter ◆ 5

THE ROMAN EMPIRE

COMMENTARY

With resources unmatched in earlier periods of Roman history, Octavian began a much needed reorganization of the Roman state. In so doing, he shaped Rome to his own concept of administrative efficiency while keeping the true power of the state in his own hands. A carefully conceived reshaping of the senatorial apparatus and administrative reforms in the provinces, when coupled with specific reforms in the capital itself, became the foundations of the new governmental system. While nurturing the birth of the empire, this "Augustus" as heir to Julius Caesar had the intelligence and foresight to maintain the appearance of the republic. During this time the borders of Rome remained relatively secure and protected by a large standing army. Roman civilization stretched to the far reaches of the Mediterranean world.

Augustus died in A.D. 14. While he lived Rome bathed in a security and stability previously unknown in her history. With his passing, new uncertainties entered the political stage and *imperator* after emperor, after Caesar, would have to come to grips with problems flowing from the succession and elevation of the ruler. It soon became apparent that the army's role and approval in these successions could not be ignored. This was most clearly demonstrated in A.D. 41 when the ignoble Claudius was placed on the throne. Though the empire would survive the Caligulas and the Neros because of the inherent stability of the administrative corps founded by Augustus, the empire was never far from chaos. Fortunately the second century saw Rome ruled effectively by five "good emperors."

This period, which ended with the reign of Marcus Auerelius, can also be referred to as the "golden age." In these centuries flourished the culture today associated with Rome. In all the fields of the arts Roman achievements can be noted. Building upon Hellenistic contributions, the Romans were able to advance many of the art forms. This is most physically notable in Roman architecture in which the Roman arch and the use of cement made it possible to accomplish sizable engineering feats, though urban housing was never the highest priority.

It is during this first century of the empire that Christianity, destined to have a profound impact on Rome and the entire world to the present day, emerged. The unique life of Jesus of Nazareth remains one of the most remarkable events in recorded history and is central to an understanding of the rise of Christianity. The work of Paul is of particular importance. Christianity, which presented a resurrected God that demanded obedience to morality, emphasized brotherhood, and promised immortality to the faithful, had wide appeal in a world increasingly riddled with insecurity and doubt. It was Paul who effectively opened the doors of Christianity to all persons. The organizational structure developed by the early Church welded the widespread Christian communities together in a way unequaled by any previous religion. In time this organizational structure encouraged the continual expansion of the Church into most areas of the empire. Although Christians had suffered occasional persecution under earlier emperors, Diocletian in 303 moved from a position of toleration to one of extreme persecution. Yet only nine years later Constantine became a true champion of Christianity. Going beyond the restoration of the Church's position in the state, Constantine, by his continuous support, firmly implanted this religion in the empire. Though still challenged by Manichaeism, a notable Persian-based religion, by the end of the fourth century, Christianity was the religion of Rome.

The very success of the church put the doctrines of Christianity into a much wider intellectual context. Inevitably widely diverse views and interpretations appeared. The most serious threat was Arianism, which challenged the divine nature of Christ and thereby cast a shadow over the church's teaching of the Trinity (God as Father, Son, and Spirit). Constantine himself dealt with these and other controversies at the Council of Nicaea in 325, but Arianism persisted.

By the third century Rome's domestic and foreign problems reached a critical point. Both problems were further underscored by notable changes in the structure, composition, and discipline of the Roman army. These so-called reforms altered the basic conditions of conscription and had far-reaching effects in society. Roman society was taking on a military look. Social mobility hardened as the ranks of the upper classes were increasingly penetrated from outside the old aristocratic order. The changes wrought in the third century set the stage for an alternating series of strong and weak rulers who attempted to hold the empire together into the fifth century.

Imperial reorganization in the fourth century would for a time stem the decay. The emperors Diocletian and Constantine are noteworthy for their efforts at reform and consolidation. Constantine's founding of the city at Byzantium, which bore his name into the fifteenth century, was an admission of the eastern threats to the empire. At the same time, Milan in northern Italy would eclipse Rome as a political center. From Milan later emperors would be able to direct their northern forces against the growing barbarian pressures.

By the end of the fourth century the empire, which had struggled against division for a century, was effectively split into a western Latin and eastern Greek civilization. Noticeably, as the last century of the empire dragged on, the foundations of the Medieval style emerged. The only unifying factor remaining in the west was the Christian church; and at Constantinople a distinct eastern civilization (Byzantine) became the basis for life there for the next thousand years.

As Rome declined, the vitality of its culture slowed. Cultural developments during this last phase relied on preserving the works of earlier periods and, at times, on expressions of religious and political propaganda. The exception is the work of Christian writers such as Jerome and Augustine who, as Church prestige rose, sought to explain in detail the origins upon which the institution had been built. In establishing this Christian view, these and other of the church fathers established the theological foundations of the next era in the development of Western civilization.

IDENTIFICATIONS

Identify each one of the following as used in the text. Refer to the text as necessary.

	Text Page
Sallust	111
jus gentium and *jus naturale*	111
Lucretius	111
Commodus	114
alimenta	116
Hadrian	117
coloni	117
Paul of Tarsus	120-121
"takers" of unique positions	122
Parthians	123
honestiores and *humiliores*	125
tetrarchy	125-126
Manichaeans	127
Julian "the Apostate"	129
Huns	129
Theodosius	129
Arias of Alexandria	131
Council of Nicaea	131
Vulgate	132
Confessions	132
The City of God	132

Map Exercise A

The Roman Empire encompassed all or part of approximately twenty-five modern states. List and locate these states with their present boundaries.

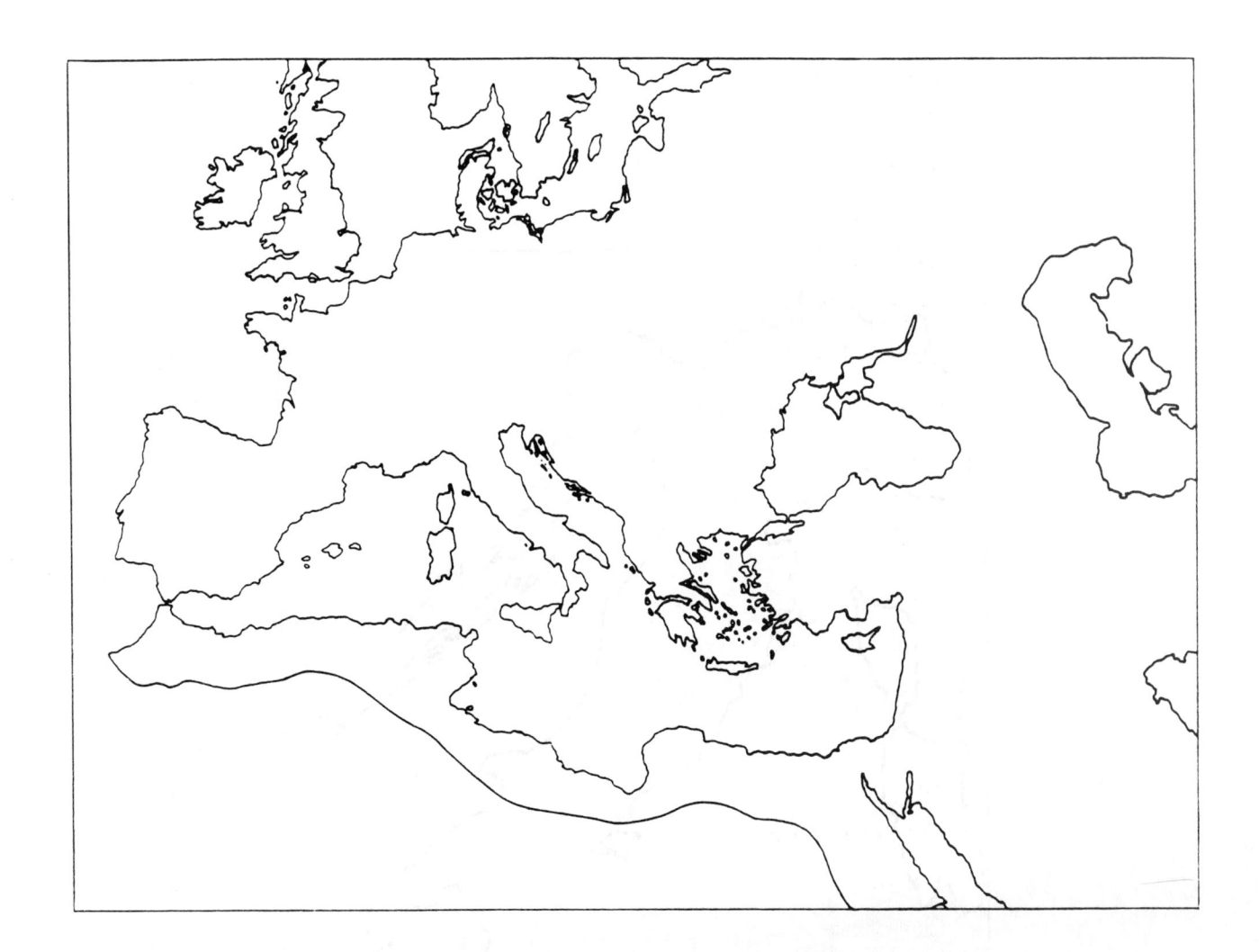

Chapter 5
The Roman Empire

Map Exercise B

On this outline map of Italy/Sicily locate each of the following cities:

1. Bologna
2. Brescia
3. Florence
4. Genoa
5. Messina
6. Milan
7. Naples
8. Rome
9. Syracuse
10. Trieste
11. Turin
12. Venice

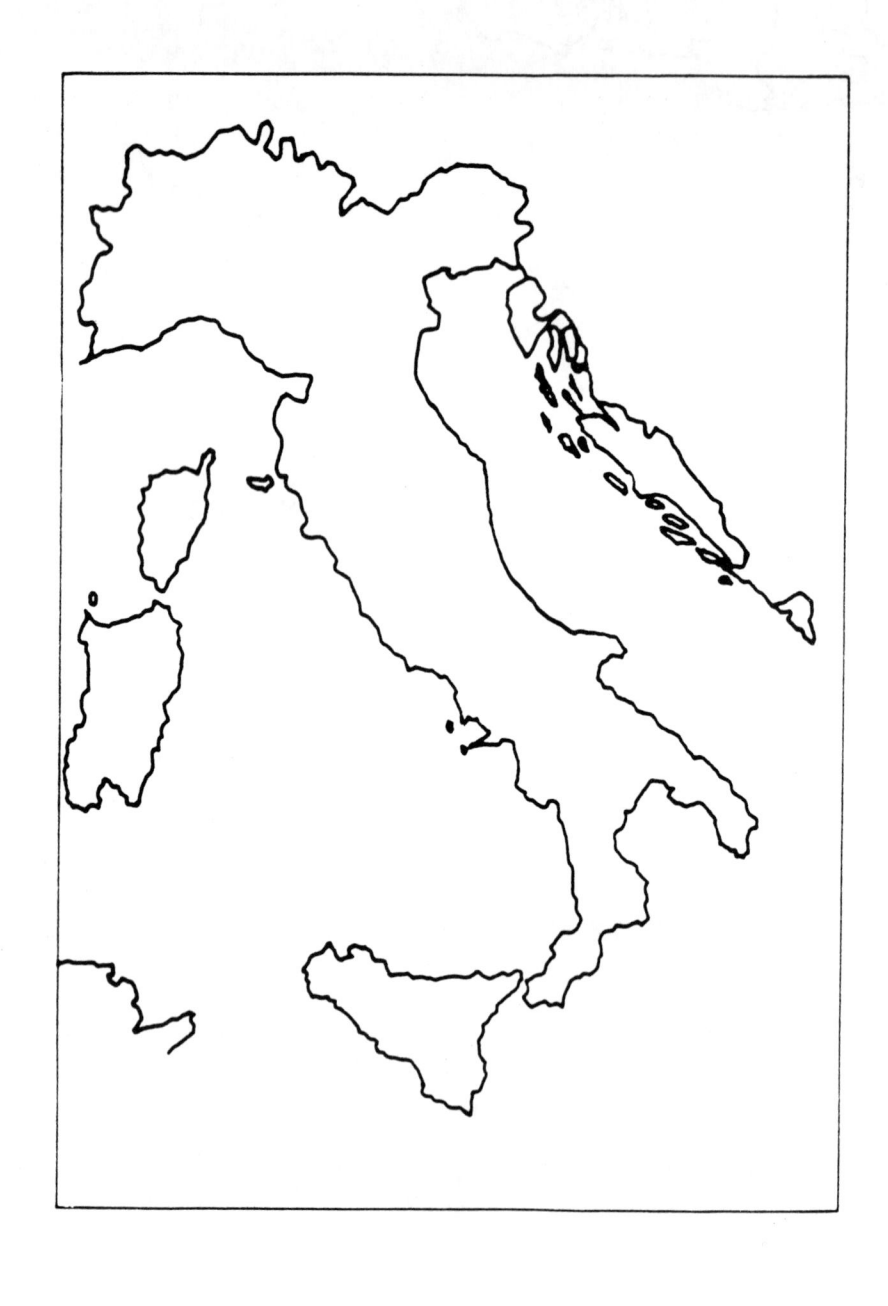

Short-Answer Exercises

Multiple-Choice

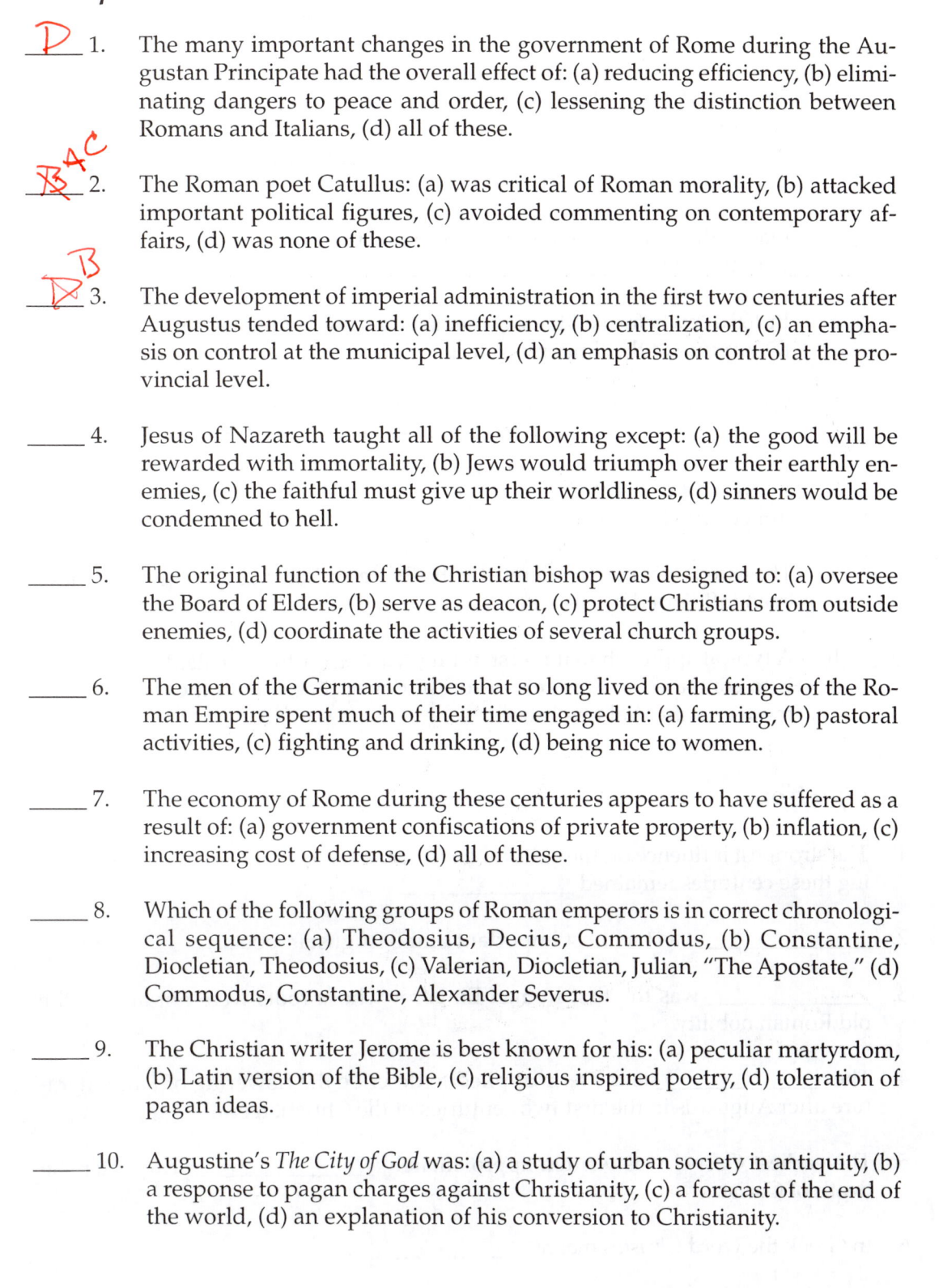

__D__ 1. The many important changes in the government of Rome during the Augustan Principate had the overall effect of: (a) reducing efficiency, (b) eliminating dangers to peace and order, (c) lessening the distinction between Romans and Italians, (d) all of these.

__B__ *AC* 2. The Roman poet Catullus: (a) was critical of Roman morality, (b) attacked important political figures, (c) avoided commenting on contemporary affairs, (d) was none of these.

__D__ *B* 3. The development of imperial administration in the first two centuries after Augustus tended toward: (a) inefficiency, (b) centralization, (c) an emphasis on control at the municipal level, (d) an emphasis on control at the provincial level.

_____ 4. Jesus of Nazareth taught all of the following except: (a) the good will be rewarded with immortality, (b) Jews would triumph over their earthly enemies, (c) the faithful must give up their worldliness, (d) sinners would be condemned to hell.

_____ 5. The original function of the Christian bishop was designed to: (a) oversee the Board of Elders, (b) serve as deacon, (c) protect Christians from outside enemies, (d) coordinate the activities of several church groups.

_____ 6. The men of the Germanic tribes that so long lived on the fringes of the Roman Empire spent much of their time engaged in: (a) farming, (b) pastoral activities, (c) fighting and drinking, (d) being nice to women.

_____ 7. The economy of Rome during these centuries appears to have suffered as a result of: (a) government confiscations of private property, (b) inflation, (c) increasing cost of defense, (d) all of these.

_____ 8. Which of the following groups of Roman emperors is in correct chronological sequence: (a) Theodosius, Decius, Commodus, (b) Constantine, Diocletian, Theodosius, (c) Valerian, Diocletian, Julian, "The Apostate," (d) Commodus, Constantine, Alexander Severus.

_____ 9. The Christian writer Jerome is best known for his: (a) peculiar martyrdom, (b) Latin version of the Bible, (c) religious inspired poetry, (d) toleration of pagan ideas.

_____ 10. Augustine's *The City of God* was: (a) a study of urban society in antiquity, (b) a response to pagan charges against Christianity, (c) a forecast of the end of the world, (d) an explanation of his conversion to Christianity.

True-False

___F___ 1. Under the emperor Augustus the frontier army of Rome was maintained at just under one million men.

___F___ 2. Because of its theme, Ovid's most popular work was the *Ars Amatoria*.

___F___ 3. Nero, despite his other shortcomings, was the first Roman emperor to take the offensive against the barbarians.

___T___ 4. The Romans invented concrete.

_____ 5. One of the great problems facing the early Christians was their relationship with the Jews.

_____ 6. In 260 a newly formed Persian-Iranian dynasty humiliated the Romans with the capture of the Emperor Valerian.

_____ 7. With the accession of the Emperor Septimius Severus at the end of the second century it is clear that Rome was becoming a military monarchy.

_____ 8. By the end of the third century the Roman army is considered to be controlled largely by mercenaries.

_____ 9. The acceptance of Christianity by the Emperor Galerius may very well have been influenced by his wife.

_____ 10. A typical approach to understanding reasons for the so-called fall of Rome is to compare the Empire's historical development with the events of the modern industrial revolution.

Completion

1. The strongest influence on the cultural development and civilization of Rome during these centuries remained _____.

2. _____ was the most important of the Augustan poets.

3. _____ was the first Roman Emperor whose roots were not among the old Roman nobility.

4. The _____ is the term applied to describe the flowering of Latin literature after Augustus in the first two centuries of the Christian era.

5. The earliest Gospel was written approximately _____ years after the death of Christ.

6. In Greek the word *Christos* means _____.

7. The origins of today's Catholic Mass can be found in the ceremonies known in the early Christian era as _____ and _____.

8. Near A.D. 250 the Emperor _____ ordered the first major persecution of the Christians.

9. The culture centered in the eastern portions of the late Roman Empire came to be called _____.

10. The priest Arius ushered in a long-standing religious controversy by challenging the Church's teaching on the _____.

FOR FURTHER CONSIDERATION

1. Describe the political arrangements of the Augustan Principate. How did Augustus deal with the Roman Senate and what effect did this relationship have on the later development of the Empire?

2. Rome was an empire and based its imperial needs on maintaining control of the provinces. What were Rome's policies toward the provinces during this era? Cite specific examples.

3. What were the basic teachings of Jesus of Nazareth? Trace the progress and growth of Christianity from its origins in the first century as an obscure eastern sect to becoming the religion of Rome in the fourth century.

4. With considerable effort the Roman Empire struggled against internal problems and external threats during the fourth and fifth centuries. In your opinion if the republic had not been replaced by the empire in the Age of Augustus could Rome have withstood these later pressures? Discuss your answer fully.

5. Based on your reading and what you have heard in class, what are the causes of the decline and "fall" of the Roman Empire?

Answers

Chapter 5
The Roman Empire

Multiple-Choice

		Text Page
1.	D	109-110
2.	C	111
3.	B	113-116
4.	B	119-120
5.	D	121
6.	C	123
7.	D	124
8.	C	*passim*/108
9.	B	132
10.	B	132

True-False

1.	F	109
2.	F	112
3.	F	113
4.	F	118
5.	T	120
6.	T	123
7	T	124
8.	T	125
9.	T	128
10.	F	133

Completion

1.	Greek/Hellenistic	110
2.	Vergil	112
3.	Vespasian	114
4.	Silver Age	117
5.	forty	118
6.	Messiah	120
7.	*agape*/love feast, *Eucharist*/thanksgiving	121
8.	Decius	127
9.	Byzantine	130
10.	Trinity	131

◆◆◆◆◆◆

From Chapters 1-5

For Further Consideration of the Documents

Each of the following questions is designed to help you reach a better understanding of the original documents presented in the last five chapters of the text. Feel free to use the page numbers provided to refer back to the document as necessary. The value of a primary historical source should not be underestimated; it helps us understand the nature of the era in which it was written.

Babylonian Story of the Flood (pp. 8-9)
1. List and briefly comment on the similarities and differences between this Babylonian Epic and the story of Noah in the Old Testament Book of Genesis?

The Development of the Athenian *Polis* (pp. 36-37)
2. "Deep was their trouble and discontent at abandoning their houses and the hereditary temples of the ancient constitution, and at having to change their habits of life and to bid farewell to what each regarded as his native city." Reflect on this statement by considering contemporary dislocations of citizens around the world?

Xenophon on Chaos in Greece (p. 59)
3. What is that Xenophon the historian saw that "invited" the Macedonian conquest.

Roman Women Make Demands (pp. 94-95)
4. Compare and contrast the demands voiced in the Roman Republic with contemporary political and economic demands of women around the world today.

Juvenal on Urban Life (p. 119)
5. List the modern equivalents of the urban dangers Juvenal presents in this passage.

THE EARLY MIDDLE AGES (476-1000): THE BIRTH OF EUROPE

COMMENTARY

The Middle Ages, or Medieval world, were formed from a mixture of Roman, Germanic, and Christian cultures. During the early Middle Ages, Europe was confronted by hostile neighbors from several quarters and well before the fall of the Roman Empire was diverting considerable attention and money to these threats. Western Europe was eventually conquered by these militarily superior tribes, whose members offered little in the way of culture and remained content to be absorbed by that of Rome. In the eastern portions of Europe and initially throughout much of the Middle East a distinct Byzantine culture developed around the great city of Constantinople. Although often beset by external pressures and internal demands, Byzantine civilization was a vast urban-concentrated organization. The now conventional religious presence of Christianity radiated from Constantinople and served as a stabilizing influence for nearly a thousand years. Until the fifteenth century the Byzantines countered the growth of the Islamic religion while maintaining a religious orthodoxy within the confines of their shrinking empire.

On the southern fringe of the Mediterranean a dynamic new force, Islam, arose eventually to challenge Western European and eastern Byzantine civilizations. The nature of the teachings of Muhammad assured many converts. After the prophet Muhammad's death, the faith of Islam spread dramatically across the entire southern tier of the old Roman Empire. That expansion was driven by the inner dynamics of the new religion and was successful because of the many divisions existing between the Eastern and Western societies. Those civilizations were forced into a position of isolation in reaction to the swift success of Islam. Within that framework a culture uniquely Western was being nurtured. The larger land units, particularly those of the great lords and the Catholic Church, became the localized centers of political, economic, and social life.

Initially dominant was the one organization that had modeled its administration on that of the Empire—the Church. At the head of the Church was the father, or pope, in Rome, who ruled over a comparatively well-organized bureaucracy and the only literate elite in Europe. Great discipline and devotion were further derived through the monastic movement, which gave the Church a certain stability that any monarch could envy. This early and solid foundation gave the Church its power and influence in later centuries. At the same time, differences between organizational and leadership styles did develop between the Western and Eastern churches.

In the west the Frankish Merovingians were the first to establish a medieval style of monarchy. By the eighth century, burdened with internal division and by Frankish custom, the Merovingians were eclipsed by the Carolingians. No greater example of monarchial success can be found in the early Middle Ages than the Carolingian ruler Charlemagne. An interesting personality by any standard, his rule immeasurably raised the prestige of the West (and himself) in the eyes of the world. His coronation as a

Roman Emperor (Holy Roman Emperor) further illuminated his elevated position. The organization of his kingdom, with its emphasis on central authority ruling through local administrators (counts), was a clear sign of the tension in medieval society between central and local authority—tension that was not fully resolved for centuries. Despite this problem, Charlemagne's era ushered in something of an intellectual revolution. For the first time in centuries an interest in the ancient works was noticeable.

Of importance also were the changes affecting the agricultural system. They had the effect of stratifying medieval society during this period and led to a harshly regulated condition of serfdom. Serfs in the difficult times following the collapse of Rome had effectively traded their freedom for security under the protection of one lord or another. They were soon locked into the often difficult and never-ending routine of servitude in which the rewards were few and the punishment severe. Parish priests chosen from among that class to administer to the serfs fared little better.

With the great king's passing, the Carolingian Empire was beset by the problems burning beneath the surface while he lived. Charlemagne's Frankish universalism was undermined by regionalism and the petty jealousies of the counts who ruled locally on behalf of the king. The sons of Louis the Pious soon divided their grandfather's kingdom into thirds according to Frankish tradition and thereby set the stage for the continual fragmentation of the empire.

The early medieval world created a complicated arrangement of the land within an equally complicated system of escalating personal, religious, and political loyalties. At the bottom of feudal society was the serf. At the top was the monarch, who ruled all. In between was an array of local chiefs who, as necessary, served their superiors though not always with the devotion hoped for. Always they had a life-death influence over their serfs. This arrangement provided sufficient security for large numbers of people and as such by the ninth century had become a settled way of life.

IDENTIFICATIONS

Identify each one of the following as used in the text. Refer to the text as necessary.

	Text Page
Emperor Valens	138
Romulus Augustulus	139
Emperor Justinian	140-141
Empress Theodora	140-141
Monophysitism	140
Corpus Juris Civilis	140
iconoclasm	141
Battle of Manzikert	141
Emperor Leo III	141/146
Muhammed	143
Mecca	143
Qur an	143
Ka'ba	143
ulema	144
Kharijites	144
"partisans of Ali"	144
Sunnis	144
manorialism	147
feudalism	147
Pachomius	148
Benedict of Nursia	149
Pope Stephen II	150-151
Donation of Constantine	152
mallus	155
missi dominici	155
"Carolingian Renaissance"	155-156
manors	156
Charles "the Bald"	158
Treaty of Verdun	158
vikings	158
fealty	159

Map Exercise A

Delineate the extent of the boundaries of the Byzantine, Muslim and Western European areas at the year 1000.

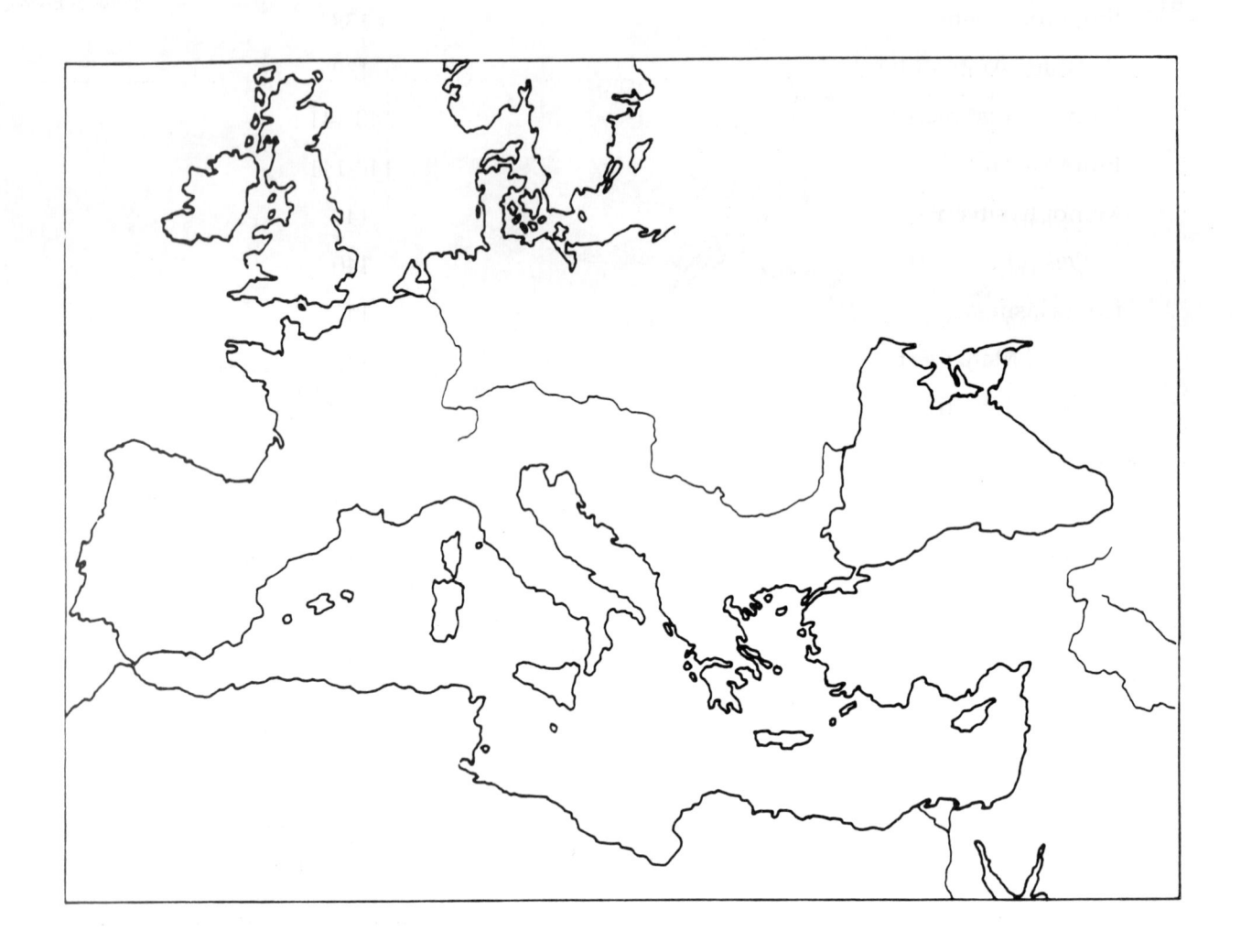

MAP EXERCISE B

On the accompanying map mark the boundaries of the Treaty of Verdun of 843. Be sure to mark the boundaries of the kingdoms of Charles the Bald, Lothar, and Louis the German.

CHAPTER 6
THE EARLY
MIDDLE AGES
(476-1000): THE
BIRTH OF EUROPE

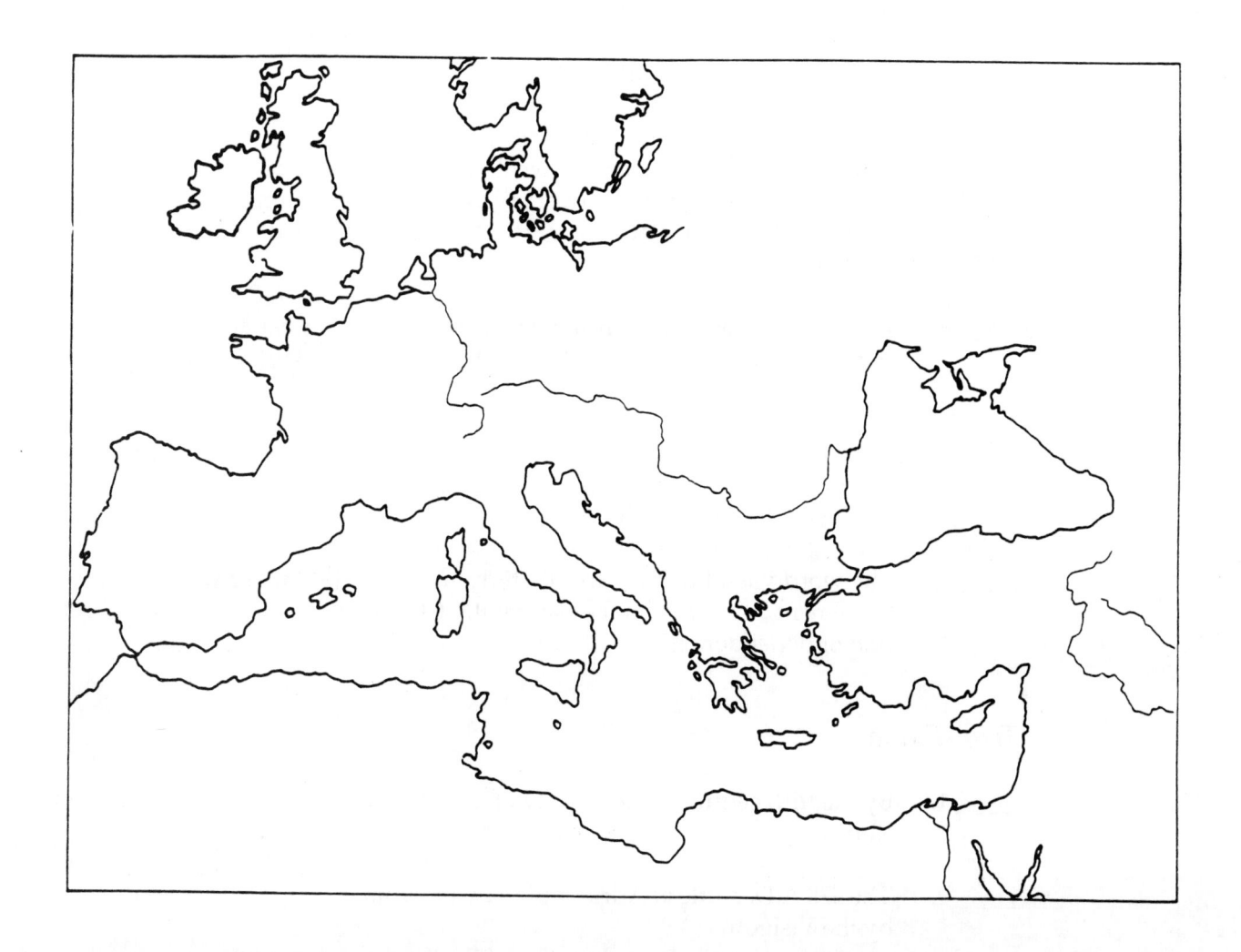

SHORT-ANSWER EXERCISES

Multiple Choice

1. The city of, (a) Naples, (b) Milan, (c) Ravenna, (d) Constantinople, was never a center of the government of the Roman Empire.

2. The section of Justinian's law code that contained his decrees was the: (a) Code, (b) *Novellae*, (c) Digest, (d) Institutes.

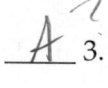

3. Which of the following is the least correct about the practice of the Islamic faith? (a) charity is forbidden, (b) polygamy is permitted, (c) eating pork is forbidden, (d) there is no clear distinction between the clergy and the laity.

4. Originally, persons who became monks were: (a) both men and women, (b) hermits, (c) sophists, (d) converted Muslims.

5. As a result of multi-sided struggle in the middle of the Eighth century: (a) Carolingian kings gained an important relationship with the Roman Church, (b) the eastern Emperor lost influence in the West, (c) Popes gained the title of "patrician of the Romans" and the Papal States, (d) all of these are correct. [marked D]

6. As Europe's best scholars, which of the following was *not* invited to Charlemagne's capital at Aachen: (a) Alcuin of York, (b) Anthony of Egypt, (c) Einhard, (d) Theodulf of Orleans. [marked B]

7. Which of the following is the most accurate statement about the feudal system? (a) serfs spent most of the week working the lord's fields, (b) the scratch plow was an improvement over the moldboard plow, (c) all peasants (serfs) were equal, (d) the status of peasants was determined by the size of their land holdings. [marked D]

8. Which of the following brothers was not involved in the settlement known as the Treaty of Verdun? (a) Pepin, (b) Charles the Bald, (c) Louis the German, (d) Lothar. [marked A or B]

9. Probably the darkest period of this era was: (a) the latter part of the eighth century, (b) the ninth century, (c) the last quarter of the ninth century and the first half of the tenth century, (d) all of these. [marked C]

10. The word vassal derives from a term meaning: (a) "those who serve," (b) "tenement," (c) "monetary payment," (d) "freemen in a contractual relation of dependence." [marked A]

True-False

1. By the fifth century A.D. the city of Constantinople was in effect the "New Rome." [T]

2. The 378 A.D. battle at Adrianople saw the Roman Emperor Valens defeated by the Visigoths. [T]

3. The word Islam means, "partisans of Ali." [F]

4. The *Hegira* of 622 marks the beginning of the Muslin calendar. [T]

5. The most moderate of the Muslim divisions are the Shi'a. [F]

6. Popes Damasus, Leo I and Gelasius I are all associated with the idea of a papal primacy centered in Rome. [T]

7. One of the major issues separating the eastern and western churches was the adoption by the west of the so-called *filioque* clause which in effect made Christ equal to God the Father. [T]

8. Charles Martel's victory at Poitiers stemmed the Muslim advance into Western Europe. [T]

___F___ 9. Charles Martel was Charlemagne's father.

___F___ 10. In feudal terminology a "liege lord" was the individual to whom a particular vassal owed the most money.

Completion

1. Despite the controversy involved, the Monophysites were supported by the Empress _____.

2. The city of Mecca is located in the modern nation of _____.

3. One of the key events in Muhammad's life was his flight from Mecca to Medina, which is known to Muslims as the _____.

4. Islam's greatest authority on Aristotle was the philosopher known in the west as _____.

5. The father of hermit monasticism was _____.

6. The concept of _____ held that the authority of the Bishop of Rome was unassailable.

7. The founder of the Merovingian dynasty was _____.

8. Charles Martel's 732 A.D. victory at _____ ended Arab expansion into Western Europe.

9. The eighth century Anglo-Saxon scholar _____ was the person responsible for bringing classical and Christian learning to Charlemagne's palace school at Aachen.

10. During the Middle Ages a land grant was called _____ or _____.

FOR FURTHER CONSIDERATION

1. What were the chief issues that divided the Eastern Church (Constantinople) and the Western Church (Rome)?

2. Explain the basic characteristics of the Islamic faith. Why were the Muslims able to expand so rapidly?

3. Describe the political, social, economic, and intellectual life in Europe at the time of Charlemagne. Would you say that these descriptions reflected Roman civilization or that of Christianity?

4. Discuss the problems of the Carolingian succession after the death of Charlemagne. How did these problems lead to the Treaty of Verdun? What have been the modern implications of this treaty?

5. Describe in detail what you consider the key factors in the transition of western Europe from the Roman Empire to the early Middle Ages.

Answers

Multiple-Choice

		Text Page
1.	A	136
2.	B	140
3.	A	143
4.	B	147
5.	A	150
6.	B	156
7.	D	156
8.	A	158
9.	C	158
10.	A	159

True-False

1.	T	136
2.	T	138
3	F	143
4.	T	143
5.	F	144
6.	T	149
7.	T	150
8.	T	151
9.	F	152
10.	F	160

Completion

1.	Theodora	140
2.	Hegira	143
3.	Saudi Arabia	143
4.	Averroes	146
5.	Anthony of Egypt	148
6.	papal primacy	149
7.	King Clovis	151
8.	Poitiers	151
9.	Alcuin	156
10.	*benefice/fief*	159

◆◆◆◆◆◆◆

Chapter 7

The High Middle Ages (1000-1300): The Ascendency of the Church and the Rise of States

COMMENTARY

By the tenth century the process of medieval empire building had reached its height. Poised on the threshold of a new millennium. the German and Frankish kings were in a position of great power and prestige. In recognition of this fact the leaders of the church had learned their place at the foot of emperors. The Germanic king Otto I provides the best example of emergent monarchy. Through a carefully contrived program Otto brought the German clergy under his patronage. In 961 when he intervened on Pope John XII's behalf in Italy, his authority in ecclesiastical matters grew immeasurably at papal expense. However, this ascendency did not last a century. The eleventh century soon experienced a reversal in church-state relations. Spurred by the reform movement of Cluny, the church underwent a considerable revival. The clearest sign of the revived church's prestige came in the controversy between the German Emperor Henry IV and the reforming Cluniac Pope Gregory VII. By 1077 a European monarch had humbled himself before the Roman Pontiff. Temporarily, at least, the sandal was on the other foot. Though the relationship between states and the church remained a problem, as evidenced in the Investiture Controversy, several centuries were yet to pass before the two institutions reached a satisfactory arrangement with each other.

An even more visible sign of the church's resurgence can be found in the Crusades. The First Crusade, which started in 1096 and resulted in the capture of Jerusalem three years later, was also an important sign of the European West's power. That Crusade demonstrated to the Byzantine and Muslim worlds alike an energetic and at times fanatical new direction of the West. And it was in the West that the Crusades had the greatest effect. Though there were military successes against the Arabs and Turks, the crusading states established in the Middle East reverted to Muslim control before very long. Yet the stimulus that the Crusades represented to European commerce and trade, particularly in Mediterranean areas, should not be underestimated.

The pontificate of Innocent III placed the church on firm footings and secured this organization for two centuries. Readily enunciating the expanding power of the papacy, Innocent III dominated the early thirteenth century. He energetically crafted the papacy into a secular power to be reckoned with, thereby casting the church in the direction of the new money-based economy. This energetic pope did not hesitate to use the crusade against internal dissent. A particularly brutal instance can be found in the elimination of the Albigensians in France. This group is noteworthy because of their extreme views for their time on procreation and birth control. Innocent III sponsored the Fourth Lateran Council in 1215 which affirmed and clarified several basic church dogma, most notably that of transubstantiation. His sanctioning of the Franciscan and Dominican orders has had a lasting influence, and created the era's most popular religious figure in St. Francis who died in 1226.

The long contest for European supremacy between the two channel powers (France and England) starts here. The effects of this struggle have long-term implications for both nations.

The Norman conquest forever altered the isolated condition of English life. From the year 1066, the English people, though separated from the continent by water, would remain participants in the fate of Europe. The unique political system that developed in England by compromise was based upon a division of political power between the king and the people. Through the Magna Carta that arrangement has had a lasting effect upon Western peoples both to the east and to the west of the British Isles.

For France, the High Middle Ages were also an important era of building foundations for the future. French monarchs were almost continually able to increase their influence over wider areas of the state. In comparison to other rulers, they were quite successful in forming the basis of a future absolute monarchy.

The situation in central Europe moved Germany into fragmentation and disunion, creating a problem that the German people have remained saddled with to the present day. Part of the German problem stemmed from the fascination of German rulers with Italy. This fascination, time and time again, brought the empire into direct confrontation with the papacy. Simultaneously with these German ambitions there occurred the church's efforts to establish its primacy as the seat of a universal empire both spiritual and temporal. In Russia the thirteenth and fourteenth centuries were a period of conquest by the Mongols from Asia. The establishment of the Muscovite state creating Moscow as the political and religious center of the Russian people then followed.

IDENTIFICATIONS

Identify each one of the following as used in the text. Refer to the text as necessary.

	Text Page
Battle of Lechfeld	164
Saint Odo	166
"Peace of God"	167
college of cardinals	167
Humiliation at Canossa	168
Concordat of Worms	168
Knights Templars	171
Saladin	171
Frederick Barbarossa	171
annates and *pallium*	172
Cathars	172
Fourth Crusade	173
mendicants	173
Franciscans and Dominicans	174
Harold Godwinsson	174
Eleanor of Aquitaine	175-176
Battle of Bouvines	177
Saint Louis	179
Abbot Sugar	180
Battle of Legnano	182
Otto of Brunswick	183
Charles of Anjou	184
Prince Vladimir	184
Yaroslav the Wise	184
boyars	184
Golden Horde	184
"third Rome	185

MAP EXERCISE

CHAPTER 7
THE HIGH MIDDLE AGES
(1000-1300): THE
ASCENDENCY OF THE
CHURCH AND THE
RISE OF STATES

Locate each of the following cities on the accompanying map:

Alexandria	Rome	Antioch
Damascus	Naples	Jerusalem
Adrianople	Pisa	Cologne
Paris	London	Kiev
Dublin	Constantinople	Moscow

In addition, locate each of the following bodies of water

English Channel	Adriatic Sea
North Sea	Ionian Sea
Atlantic Ocean	Aegean Sea
Bay of Biscay	Black Sea
Strait of Gibraltar	Baltic Sea
Mediterranean Sea	Gulf of Finland

Similarly, each of the following islands or island groups:

Corsica	Balearic Islands
Sardinia	Crete
Sicily	Rhodes
Malta	Cyprus

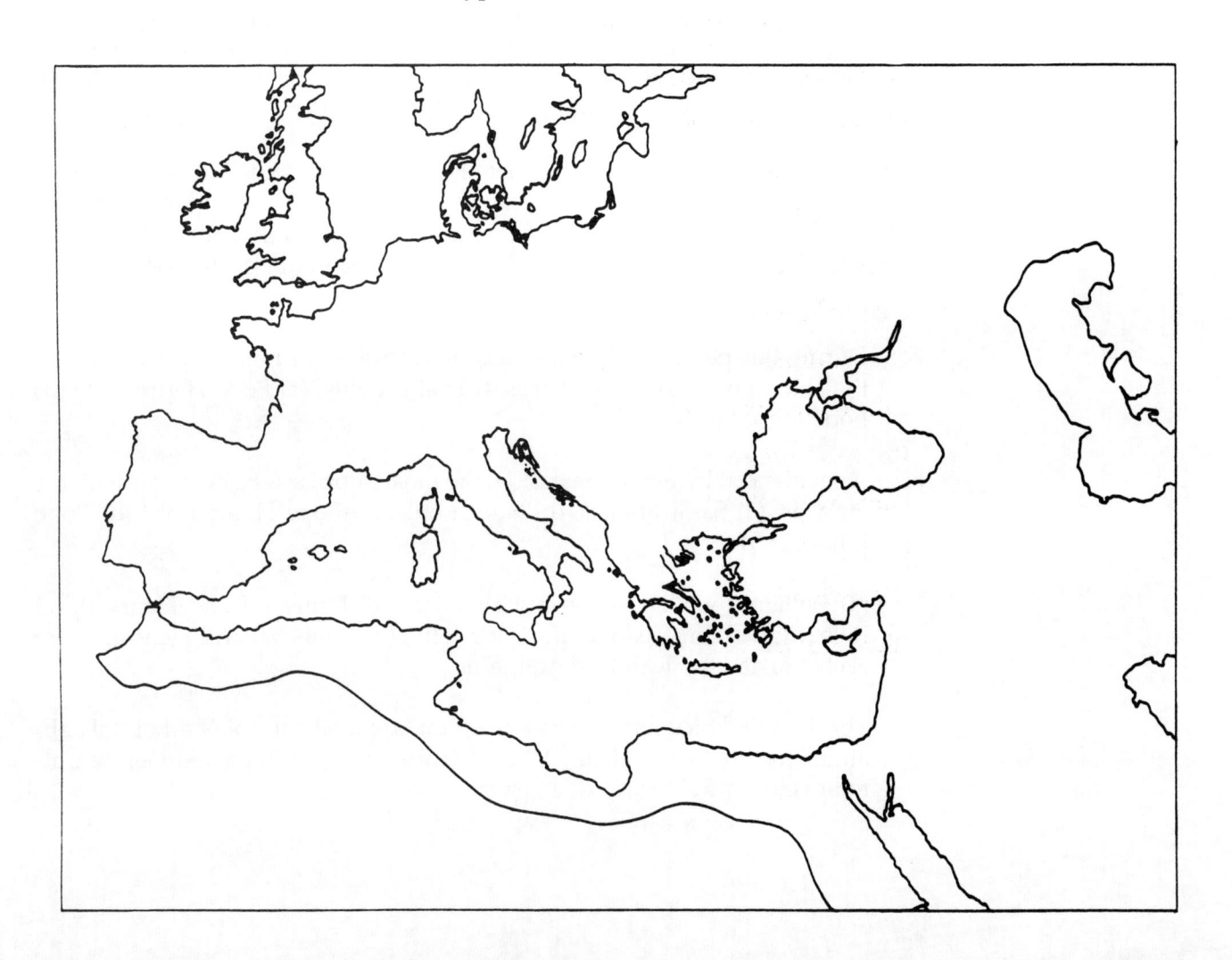

Short-Answer Exercises

Multiple-Choice

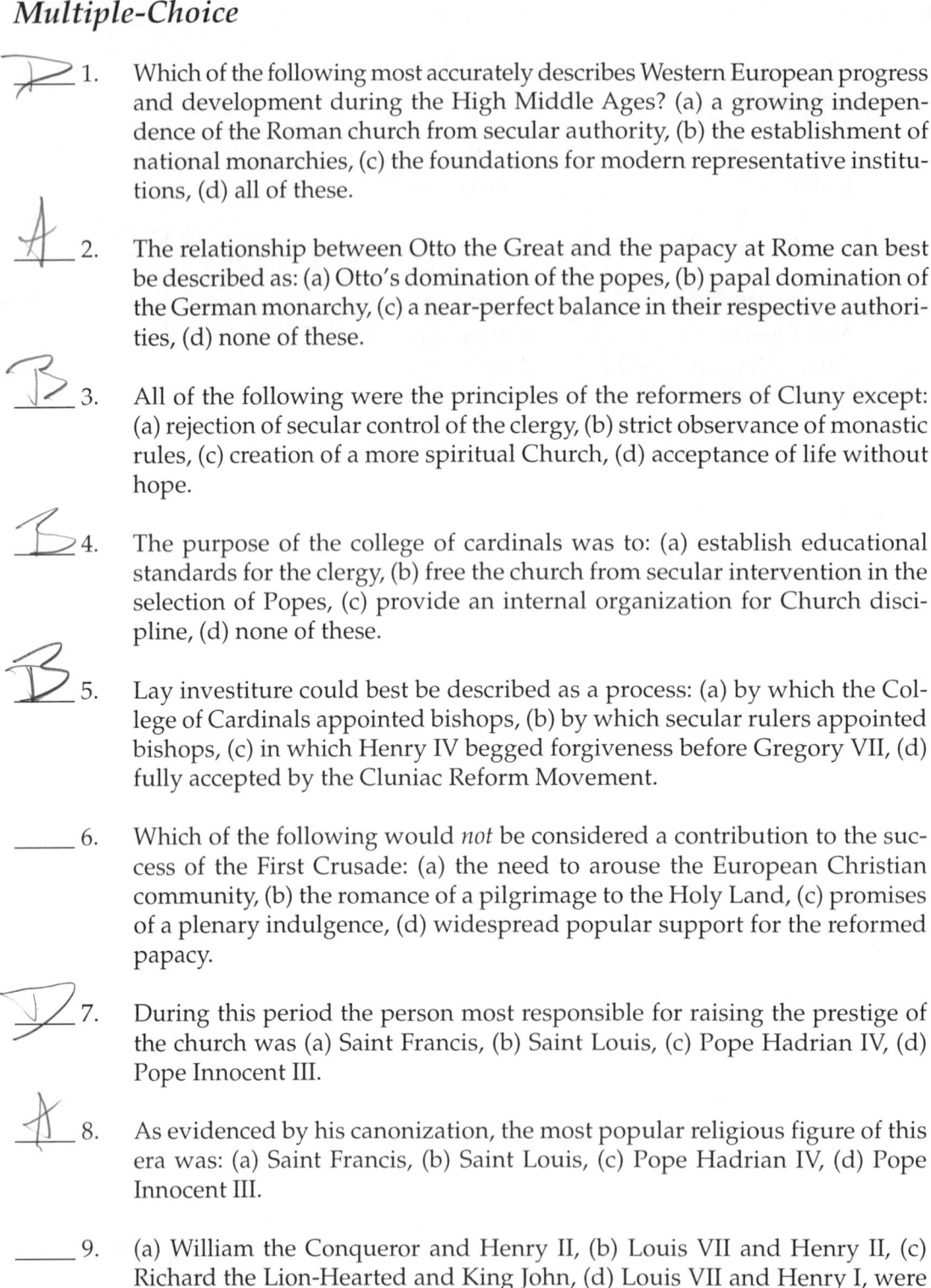

___D___ 1. Which of the following most accurately describes Western European progress and development during the High Middle Ages? (a) a growing independence of the Roman church from secular authority, (b) the establishment of national monarchies, (c) the foundations for modern representative institutions, (d) all of these.

___A___ 2. The relationship between Otto the Great and the papacy at Rome can best be described as: (a) Otto's domination of the popes, (b) papal domination of the German monarchy, (c) a near-perfect balance in their respective authorities, (d) none of these.

___B___ 3. All of the following were the principles of the reformers of Cluny except: (a) rejection of secular control of the clergy, (b) strict observance of monastic rules, (c) creation of a more spiritual Church, (d) acceptance of life without hope.

___B___ 4. The purpose of the college of cardinals was to: (a) establish educational standards for the clergy, (b) free the church from secular intervention in the selection of Popes, (c) provide an internal organization for Church discipline, (d) none of these.

___B___ 5. Lay investiture could best be described as a process: (a) by which the College of Cardinals appointed bishops, (b) by which secular rulers appointed bishops, (c) in which Henry IV begged forgiveness before Gregory VII, (d) fully accepted by the Cluniac Reform Movement.

_____ 6. Which of the following would *not* be considered a contribution to the success of the First Crusade: (a) the need to arouse the European Christian community, (b) the romance of a pilgrimage to the Holy Land, (c) promises of a plenary indulgence, (d) widespread popular support for the reformed papacy.

___D___ 7. During this period the person most responsible for raising the prestige of the church was (a) Saint Francis, (b) Saint Louis, (c) Pope Hadrian IV, (d) Pope Innocent III.

___A___ 8. As evidenced by his canonization, the most popular religious figure of this era was: (a) Saint Francis, (b) Saint Louis, (c) Pope Hadrian IV, (d) Pope Innocent III.

_____ 9. (a) William the Conqueror and Henry II, (b) Louis VII and Henry II, (c) Richard the Lion-Hearted and King John, (d) Louis VII and Henry I, were each married to Eleanor of Aquitaine.

_____ 10. The so-called Sicilian Connection led to: (a) papal control of all of Italy, (b) an alliance between Henry VI and Innocent III, (c) repeated German attempts to control Sicily, (d) a general European war.

True-False

_____ 1. In the tenth century Popes ruled at the pleasure of Otto the Great.

_____ 2. The encouragement of clerical marriage was an important driving force of the Cluniac Reform Movement.

_____ 3. Uncompromising greed was the chief inspiration for the early Crusades.

_____ 4. During this period of history Bernard of Clairvaux was probably the most influential monastic leader.

_____ 5. The Fourth Lateran Council formalized the sacrament of Penance (Reconciliation) as a central means of religious discipline.

_____ 6. In reality the English Magna Carta of 1215 had no long term effect.

_____ 7. Upon his accession to the throne France's Louis VII turned against Church influence there.

_____ 8. The French king Louis IX's successes at home and abroad are exclusively the result of his religious fanaticism.

_____ 9. The German king Frederick I's efforts against Arnold of Brescia restored Pope Adrian IV's position in Italy.

_____ 10. The military resistance of the Princes of Moscow allowed them to make that city the "Third Rome" in the eyes of the Russian people.

Completion

1. In the tenth century Otto the Great's father, _____, placed his son in a strong territorial position.

2. One of the first popes to reign without the consent of the Holy Roman Emperor was _____.

3. In 1122 the Investiture Controversy was apparently settled in the agreements of the _____.

4. Pope _____ sponsored the First Crusade.

5. _____ was the most important church meeting of this period.

6. _____ was the leading theologian of the Dominican Order.

7. In winning the battle of _____, William the Conqueror made good his claim to the English throne.

8. William the Conqueror's exact survey of England is known as the _____.

9. _____ was the most powerful and successful of the French monarchs during this era.

10. In the early period of the High Middle Ages the center of Russian political and economic development was the city of _____.

FOR FURTHER CONSIDERATION

1. How did the Lay Investiture controversy of the eleventh century reflect the medieval situation of church-state relations?

2. What were the causes of the Crusades? Were they successful? Describe the overall effect of the Crusades on Western Europe.

3. Compare and contrast the internal political development of England and France from the mid-eleventh to the mid-thirteenth century. Cite examples as necessary.

4. Compare the pontificate of Innocent III with reigns of secular rulers in the thirteenth century. How would you assess Innocent's achievements on behalf of the church in relation to achievements of secular rulers on behalf of the state?

5. Who were the Mongols? How did Mongol rule effect medieval Russia? In your opinion have the effects of this era extended into our time? Comment fully.

ANSWERS

Multiple-Choice

		Text Page
1.	D	*passim*
2.	A	164
3.	D	166
4.	B	167
5.	B	167
6.	A	169
7.	D	172
8.	A	174
9.	B	176
10.	C	182

True-False

1.	T	165
2.	F	167
3	F	169
4.	T	171
5.	T	173
6.	T	176
7.	F	178
8.	F	180
9.	T	182
10.	F	185

Completion

1.	Henry I, the Fowler	164
2.	Pope Stephen IX	167
3.	Concordat at Worms	168
4.	Urban II	169
5.	Fourth Lateran Council	173
6.	St. Thomas Aquinas	174
7.	Hastings	174
8.	Domesday Book	174-175
9.	Philip Augustus	178-179
10.	Kiev	184

◆ ◆ ◆ ◆ ◆ ◆ ◆

THE HIGH MIDDLE AGES (1000-1300): PEOPLE, TOWNS, AND UNIVERSITIES

COMMENTARY

By the High Middle Ages, European society was divided into four distinct classes. The hierarchical nature of society at the time saw the *nobility* and the *clergy* clearly dominant over the *peasants* and *townspeople*. Based upon the need for survival, medieval life was controlled from the top politically and religiously. For centuries each of the ranks and virtually all females had accepted their relative positions within the structure. Yet the emergence of towns with their *guilds* and their continual quest for commercial identity within a world of agriculture would soon alter the medieval landscape. By the end of this era one can observe the stirrings of social modernity.

The Crusades were the cause of a basic upheaval in European life. This upheaval would continue to affect society, the economic development, and the political character of the West for centuries to come. As demonstrated in the Fourth Crusade, Mediterranean commerce and Venice's role as a leading regional power grew directly from the activities associated with these wars. Throughout Europe new cities were born, old ones became important centers of trade and commerce. In turn these cities became the focus of a new social class whose position was based on commercial wealth instead of land. The members of that class can be described as early capitalists. They became an important feature of these centuries and their activities were fundamental to the vast changes that continue to operate in Western society. As a class between the upper and lower classes, these great merchants, and ultimately the middle class, were in the forefront as the medieval world gave way to the modern. The emergence of towns and the new classes within them was destined not only to break up feudal society but also to act as a powerful force for change.

A more academic subject of this era is the rise of the universities. Colleges at Bologna in Italy and at Paris were by the thirteenth century important centers for the spread of knowledge. These earlier works became the fundamental subjects of higher study in the Middle Ages. The student's responsibility emphasized knowledge of what had been written rather than speculation on new possibilities. In this atmosphere Scholasticism flourished. And it was not long before critics of the learning method began to offer alternatives. They rejected the rigors of the scholastic theology and emphasized more practical and professional skills. This debate between supporters of the pure liberal arts and the proponents of more vocational training can still be heard in academe today. Certainly, as the intellectual pace quickened with each new generation of university-trained scholars, the clash between philosophy and theology could not long be stilled. For almost three centuries nominalists and realists would debate the questions of reality, truth, and universals. These philosophical questions acted as a great inducement to learning. Scholars picked up the swords of nominalism and realism as eagerly and as vigorously as their crusading counterparts took the Cross.

Chapter ◆ 8

The inner dynamics of the European socio-economic structure are, on the whole, difficult to trace. Yet modern historians and sociologists increasingly are discovering the modes of living of the common people throughout the Middle Ages. As these efforts continue the veil of darkness so long associated with the medieval world will be folded away.

Physically, mentally and morally weaker than man in the eyes of the medieval church and society a woman's place was carefully circumscribed. In marriage, husbands were expected to discipline their wives. By modern standards in the West a women's choices in life were few and no doubt equally depressing. Within medieval social customs the female image and role was confusing and seemingly contradictory, particularly when compared to the veneration expected of the Virgin Mary. Equally difficult were the expectations and character assigned to medieval children. A high rate of infant mortality cautioned parents against heavy emotional investment in their infant offspring. However, by the age of seven children entered the process of learning and coping with the realities of the adult world, difficult as it undoubtedly was. Society, politics, and the changing economic life of this era reflected the general character of the Middle Ages. At the same time and over the next several centuries the people of Western Europe at every social level were living through an age of transition.

IDENTIFICATIONS

Identify each one of the following as used in the text. Refer to the text as necessary.

	Text Page
stirrup	188
courtly love	189
saeculum	190
beguine houses	191
"first estate"	191
excommunication	191
coloni	192
demesne	192
three-field system	193
"rough hewn men"	194
urban patriciate	194
sumptuary laws	195
University of Bologna	197
trivium and *quadrivium*	198
Romanesque	199
Gothic	199
Robert de Sorbon	201
the "summa"	202
Peter Abelard	202
cult of the virgin Mary	203
polygyny vs. monogamy	203
practice of infanticide	204
wergild	205

MAP EXERCISE

On the accompanying map locate each of the medieval university centers at Bologna, Paris and Oxford.

Additionally, research the names of ten major European universities and locate them on the accompanying map.

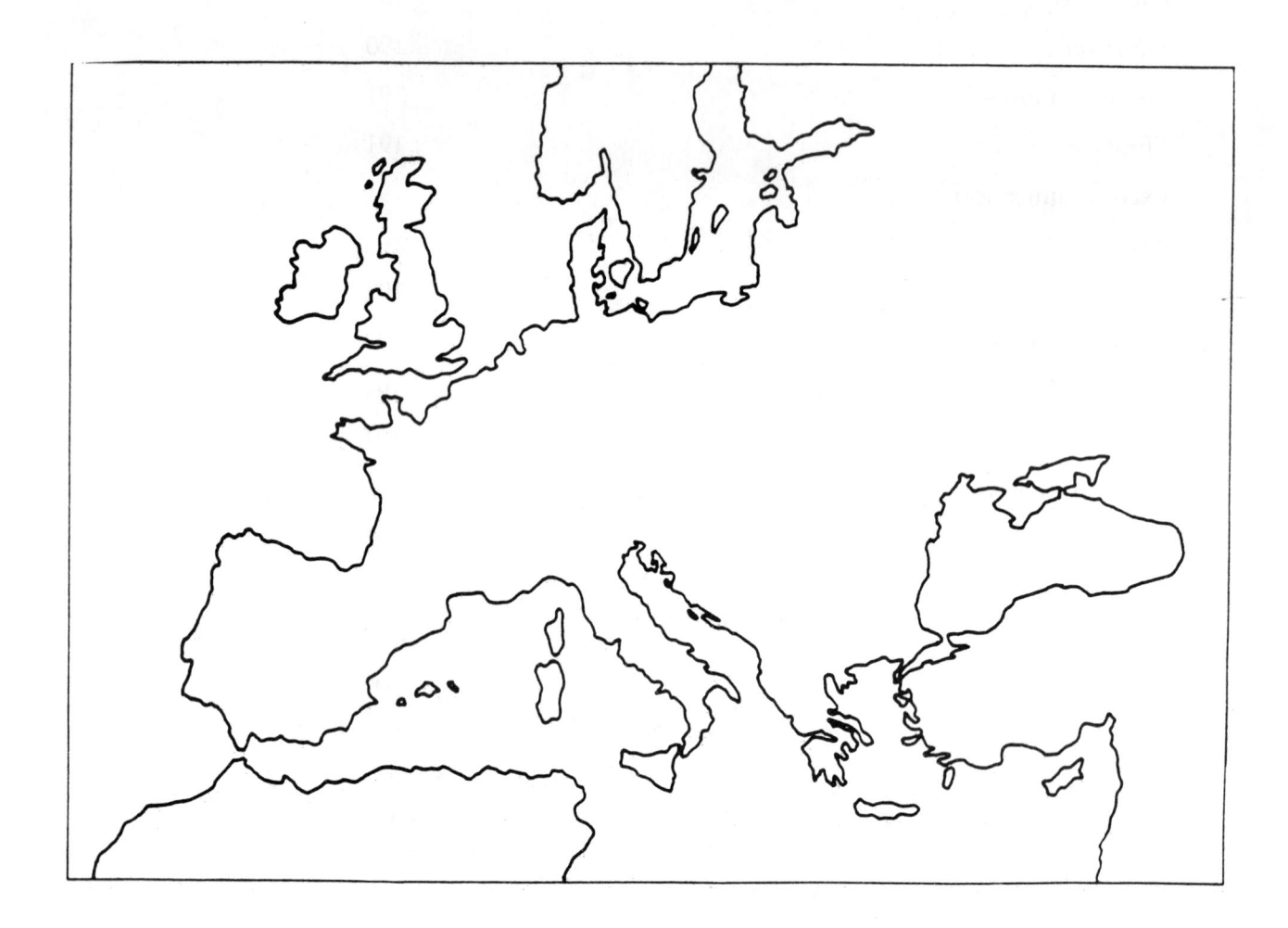

Short-Answer Exercises

Multiple-Choice

1. The pastimes of the medieval nobility during the Middle Ages were dominated by: (a) card playing and gambling, (b) fishing and drinking, (c) hunting and tournaments, (d) tournaments and carousing.

2. Courtly love can be described by each of the following except: (a) love at a distance, (b) sex without physical sex, (c) lovers who always suffered the consequences, (d) love unconsummated by sexual intercourse.

3. As contrasted with the secular clergy, the regular clergy of the Middle Ages could best be described as: (a) the least prayerful among the clergy, (b) the spiritual elite among the clergy, (c) the least respected among the clergy, (d) composed of churchmen above the rank of bishop.

4. An important means of raising money for the Church during this era was the collection of tithes which amounted to: (a) 1 percent of a person's income, (b) 10 percent of a person's income, (c) 25 percent of a person's income, (d) 50 percent of a person's income.

5. A major portion of the average peasant's life during this period revolved around: (a) farm cooperative exhibitions, (b) tournaments, (c) religion, (d) all of these.

6. The *Summa Theologica* was written by: (a) John of Salisbury, (b) William of Ockham, (c) Peter Lombard, (d) none of these.

7. Berangar of Tours was a medieval scholastic who questioned the Church's teaching on: (a) monasticism, (b) clerical celibacy, (c) the Trinity, (d) transubstantiation.

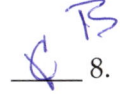

8. The image of women in medieval society might best be described as: (a) necessarily taken from Adam's side, (b) contradictory, (c) man's partner in life, (d) none of these apply.

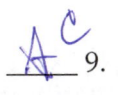

9. In this era nunneries, our modern convents, provided a place: (a) of refuge for a sinful woman, (b) for women to learn blue-collar trades, (c) of education for upper class women, (d) none of these are correct.

10. Medieval children: (a) were allowed to marry much earlier than today, (b) assumed adult responsibilities at an early age, (c) usually began schooling or apprenticing at the age of eight, (d) all of these.

True-False

1. While the nobility viewed warfare as the natural state of things, townspeople and peasants preferred peace.

2. The evolution of the modern concept of courtesy originally stems from the distinctive socio-religious practices of the higher clergy.

_____ 3. During this period of European history it is estimated that as much as 15 percent of the population were clerics.

_____ 4. It is noted that by the eleventh century only about 5 percent of the population lived in an urban setting.

_____ 5. In this era the largest towns in Europe would be found in France.

_____ 6. Thanks to the Muslim scholars of Spain many of the works of the classical era Greeks were preserved and often translated into Latin.

_____ 7. Because of differing construction techniques, Gothic structures, primarily cathedrals, were much brighter than Romanesque structures.

_____ 8. The art of discovering a truth by finding the contradictions in arguments against it is called rhetoric.

_____ 9. In the Middle Ages impoverished knights were known as "weaker vessels."

_____ 10. For Carolingian women of the ninth and tenth centuries, monogamy had its price.

Completion

1. The ceremonial entrance into the noble class was called _____.

2. The once great power of the _____ declined as a result of several factors ranging from loss of population to changes in military tactics during the fourteenth century.

3. The monastic style established by _____ was an important factor in the growth and success of the medieval monasteries.

4. Though medieval lords were probably less severe in their control over the serfs than we might think, they had the right to exact what we might call today nuisance taxes, known as _____.

5. Within the medieval cities competing _____ developed primarily to enhance the business interests of members.

6. Medieval towns enjoyed a certain degree of _____; but after the fourteenth century they would be under the increasing domination of their rulers.

7. The first important Western university was founded at _____.

8. Unlike today medieval _____ appear to have had much greater control over lecture topics, the quality of their professors and school costs.

9. The college system first developed at the University of _____.

10. The standard textbook for medieval theology was Peter Lombard's _____.

FOR FURTHER CONSIDERATION

1. As you imagine it, describe what medieval life was like for each of the four social classes: nobility, clergy, townspeople, and peasants.

2. What effect did towns have on late medieval life? Explain in detail how each of the classes were effected?

3. Based on your understanding of the medieval experience what suggestions would you make for improving or changing higher education today?

4. How would you assess the position of women within each of the classes of medieval society? How were their roles and functions similar to and different from those of women in previous ages and those of women in modern times?

5. Describe the life of children in this period of the Middle Ages. Compare and contrast with modern theories of child rearing, and with your own views.

Answers

Multiple-Choice

		Text Page
1.	C	189
2.	C	189
3.	B	190-191
4.	B	191
5.	C	193
6.	D	202
7.	D	202
8.	B	203
9.	C	204
10.	D	204-205

True-False

1.	T	188
2.	F	189
3.	F	191
4.	T	194
5.	F	194
6.	T	197
7.	T	199
8.	F	201
9.	F	203
10.	T	204

Completion

1.	knighthood	188
2.	nobility	190
3.	St. Benedict	190
4.	*banalities*	192
5.	guilds	196
6.	autonomy/freedom/ independence	197
7.	Bologna	197
8.	students	197
9.	Paris	201
10.	*Four Books of Sentences*	202

◆ ◆ ◆ ◆ ◆ ◆

Chapter 9

THE LATE MIDDLE AGES (1300-1527): CENTURIES OF CRISIS

COMMENTARY

The view of the late Middle Ages presented in this chapter is not a bright one. Too many overwrought problems between several states, rampant pestilence, and assault upon the institution of the Church from several quarters did not augur well for the people of this era. A long and exhausting war between England and France in which both struggled for supremacy, land, and cities had considerable consequences in each country. Though in the end the English threat to France was entirely reduced, the Hundred Years' War to a degree foreshadowed modern warfare.

Beyond being an important English victory, the battle of Crecy (August 1346) had two long-term effects on Western history. In one, the English longbow as a practical military weapon is fully recognized. And consequently, the longbow became, in this last era before the age of gunpowder, an effective infantry weapon which changed forever the relationship between feudal knights and their once subservient peasantry. The new weaponry was soon translated into stronger royal authority.

The Hundred Years' War also provided the backdrop for that amazing story of the great French heroine Joan of Arc, a 19-year- old at the time of her execution in 1431. Along with the ravages of war, Europeans had to contend with another scourge the effects of which went a long way toward ending the Middle Ages. The so-called "Black Death" was a widespread and ravaging assault upon European life. It started in the mid-fourteenth century and engulfed, with few exceptions, most of the cities of Europe. In an era when modern medical practice was a distant reality the assault of this vicious strain of bubonic plague was never fully understood by contemporaries, as today we cannot fully fathom its impact on them. Even Boccaccio's description (1348) cannot fully express the horrible, personal attack on one's body that was the Black Death. The contraction of the disease and the inevitability of one's own death had a telling impact on society. The social and economic effects of the plague were felt well into the sixteenth century.

As if more bad news were needed by the people of these centuries, they were also to witness a steady decline of that institution that had so long been a pillar of medieval life. Politically and spiritually the corrosion of the Roman Church was evident. From the very height of power under Pope Innocent III the fortunes of that vast international organization were reduced during the late Middle Ages. Popes and churchmen were increasingly embroiled in political battles with European rulers from which few survived without soiled hands. The struggles between several Popes, particularly Boniface VIII, and King Philip "the Fair" of France remain a classic case of the clash between spiritual and secular authority, a case to be repeated well into the next century.

Following the turmoil of, and related to the Avignon Papacy, the Church at the end of the fourteenth century was challenged afresh by secular religious movements in England and Bohemia (the modern Czech Republic). These movements challenged the worldliness of the Church and called for greater adherence to fundamental Christian principles among other serious theological disputations. At the same time the Papacy itself was directly challenged by the establishment of "Popes (anti-Popes)" at Avignon (France) and Pisa (Italy). The ensuing struggle between schismatic Popes gave rise to the concept of conciliarism—a topic of near continual debate amongst theologians and at a series of Church councils meeting well into the fifteenth century.

IDENTIFICATIONS

Identify each of the of the following as used in the text. Refer to the text as necessary.

	Text Page
"national" consciousness	208
Battle of Sluys	209
Battle of Crecy	209
Estates General	209
Peace of Bretigny	211
John Ball and Wat Tyler	211
Treaty of Troyes	211
Saint Joan	211-212
Black Death	213
flagellants	213
Decameron	214
Innocent III	216
Clericis Laicos	217
Bernard Saisset	217
Unam Sanctum	217
Guillaume de Nogaret	217-218
William of Ockham	219
Marsilius of Padua	219
"Gallican liberties"	219
Lollards and Hussites	220-221
Conciliarists	221-222
Council of Constance	221-222
Council of Basel	222

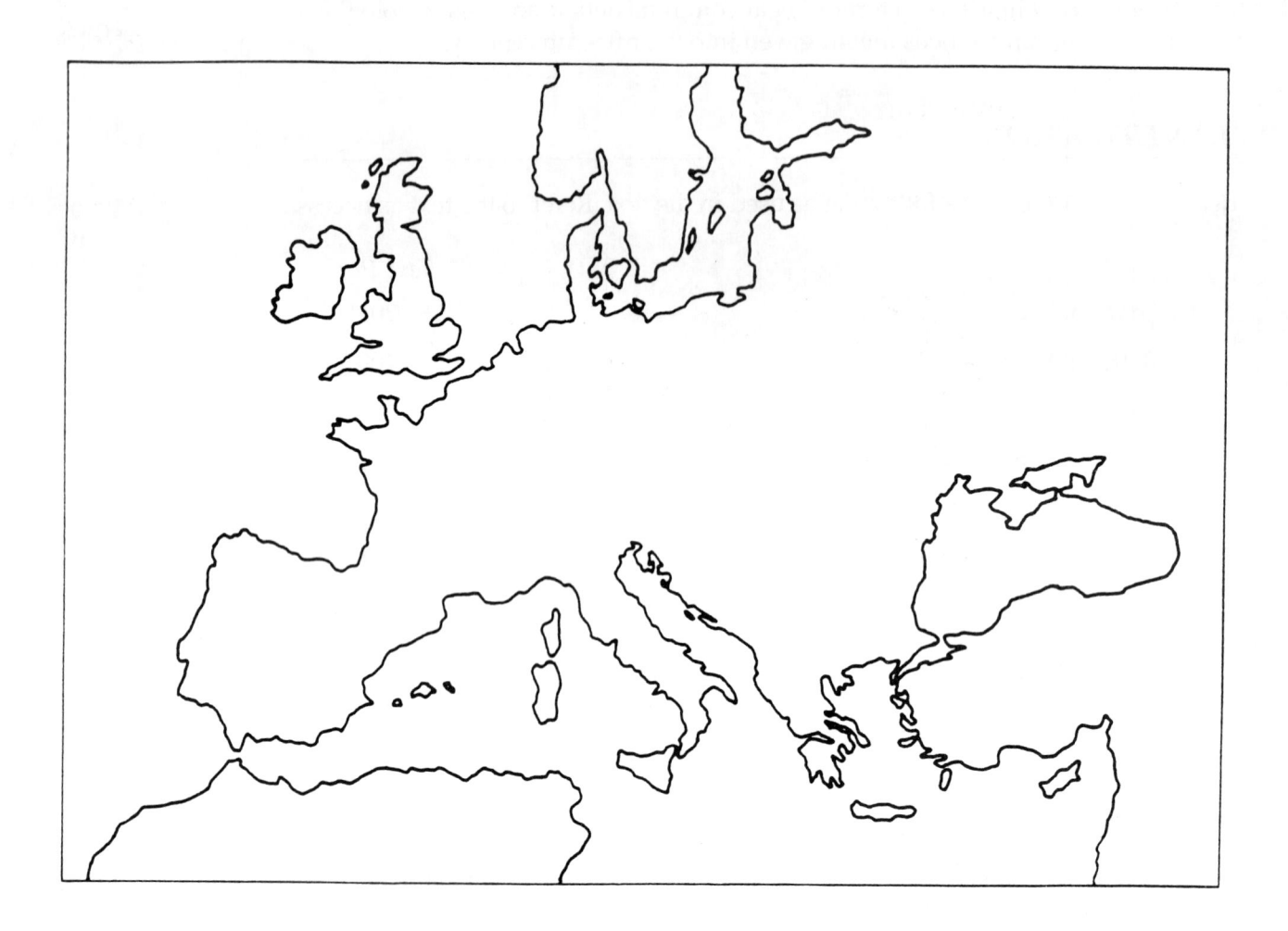

Map Exercise A

On this map of contemporary Europe, outline the extent of the spread of the Black Death during the 14th and 15th centuries.

MAP EXERCISE B

Locate each of these cities and/or Church Councils.

Avignon	Prague	London
Pisa	Constance	Paris
Oxford	Basel	Constantinople
Rome	Florence	Milan

Locate the Bay of Sluys, and the battlefield of Crecy.

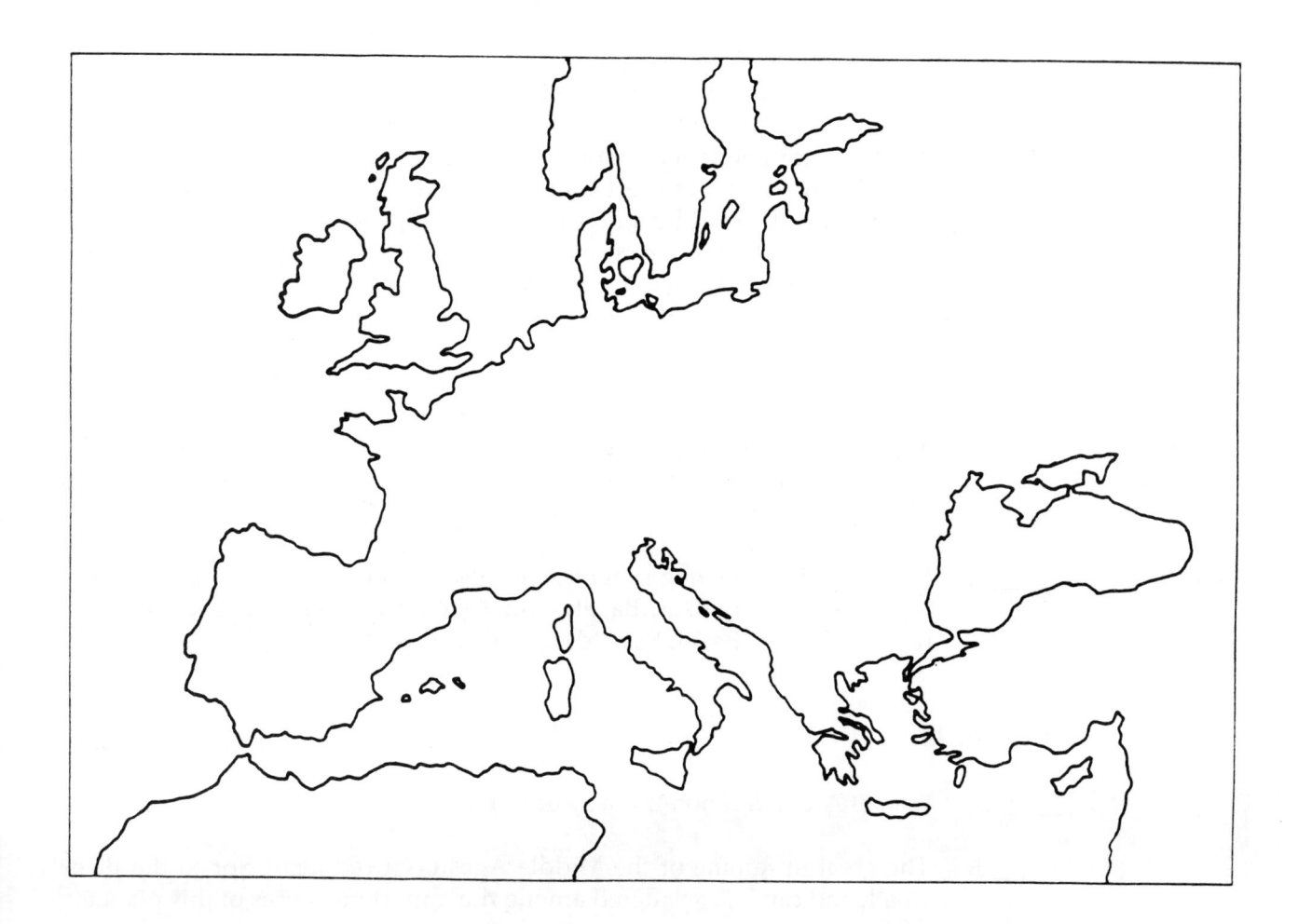

SHORT ANSWER EXERCISES

Multiple-Choice

_____ 1. The three great calamities developed in this chapter are: (a) civil war in England, the *Jacquerie* in France, and the Hussite revolt in the Empire, (b) the circumstances surrounding the execution of Joan of Arc, midterm exams, and the *Lollard* revolt in England, (c) basically war, plague and schism, (d) all of these.

_____ 2. The longbow was an effective weapon because it could: (a) reach considerable distances, (b) fire six arrows a minute when properly manned, (c) pierce armor, (d) all of these capabilities existed.

_____ 3. In reality the success of Joan of Arc was caused by: (a) divine intervention, (b) her military genius, (c) her youth, (d) her inspiration.

_____ 4. In this era the average European faced severe hunger in their lifetime: (a) once, (b) twice, (c) four times, (d) ten times.

_____ 5. As a result of the Black Death it is estimated that the western European population was reduced by: (a) 40%, (b) 50%, (c) 60%, (d) 70%.

_____ 6. Avignon is located in: (a) France, (b) Italy, (c) Germany, (d) England.

_____ 7. The clergy "ought to be content with food and clothing" is associated with: (a) John Wycliffe, (b) Pope John XXII, (c) John Huss, (d) John Ziska.

_____ 8. The basic argument of the conciliarists was that: (a) Church councils working with the Pope were best suited to lead the faithful, (b) Church councils guided and directed by a non-schismatic Pope would be best, (c) Church legislation could only be decided through a series of regionally sponsored councils, (d) Church councils, representing the whole body of the faithful, had greater authority than Popes.

_____ 9. Which of the following statements is the least correct concerning the Council of Constance: (a) passed the resolution *Sacrosancta*, (b) in 1958 Pope John XXIII declared this council to be the greatest ever convened, (c) the council made provisions for subsequent meetings on a regular basis, (d) it elected the Pope, Martin V.

_____ 10. Which of the following sequence of Church councils is in proper chronological order: (a) Pisa, Basel, Constance, (b) Basel, Pisa, Constance, (c) Constance, Basel, Pisa, (d) Pisa, Constance, Basel.

True-False

_____ 1. Joan of Arc was canonized a saint in 1456.

_____ 2. The greatest famine of the Middle Ages occurred just prior to the Black Death and can be considered among the important causes of this plague.

_____ 3. As the Black Death took its grim toll in Europe it should be noted that townspeople and the church profited.

_____ 4. Celestine V, a Calabrian hermit, can be described as a saintly but inept Pope.

_____ 5. The Papal bull of 1301 "Listen, My Son" allowed continued taxation of the clergy in France.

_____ 6. The so-called Gallican liberties permitted wide governmental control of taxation and ecclesiastical appointments in France.

_____ 7. John Ziska was an important Hussite leader in the first half of the fifteenth century.

_____ 8. Both Lollards and Hussites agreed that priest guilty of mortal sin could not perform valid sacraments.

_____ 9. The declaration *Sacrosancta* was considered the authoritative basis of the Conciliar Movement.

_____ 10. Although crisis, calamity, loss and doubt may be commonly used to describe the late medieval period of Western history; there were hopeful signs in the birth of humanism and in the increase in secular education.

Completion

1. In this period the development of the _____ gave England a clear military advantage against the French.

2. During the early stages of the Hundred Year's War France experienced a widespread popular revolt known as the _____.

3. France saw considerable territorial devastation during the war; but experienced the awakening of _____.

4. An excellent source for understanding how people reacted to the great plague of the fourteenth century can be found in Boccaccio's _____.

5. The struggle between Philip IV of France and Pope Boniface VIII is symbolic of the struggle for political power between _____ and _____ in the late Middle Ages.

6. Probably, _____ was the most powerful of the Avignon Popes.

7. Founded in the mid-fourteenth century the _____ was a center for religious reform and for a growing Czech nationalism.

8. Granted an audience at the Council of Constance, _____ was executed there for heresy in the summer of 1415.

9. The years of the Avignon Papacy can also be referred to as the _____ of the Church.

10. The papal bull _____ could be considered the final blow to the Conciliar Movement.

For Further Consideration

1. Discuss the causes, events, and significance of the Hundred Years' War. Estimate how this war affected the townspeople and peasants in both England and France. Were people affected differently in each country?

2. Describe what you consider to be the urban and rural effects of the Black Death.

3. What were the causes and effects of the Great Schism? How does the Conciliar Movement relate to the Great Schism?

4. Who were the Hussites? What were their fundamental principles? How far did the Church willingly make concessions to this movement? In your opinion, what Hussite practices/positions have made there way into modern church practices, Catholic or Protestant?

5. Give an overall assessment of these two centuries from the perspective of (1) economic progress, (2) social change, and (3) key developments within the Roman Catholic Church, especially those considered of far-reaching consequence.

Answers

Multiple-Choice

		Text Page
1.	C	207
2.	D	209
3.	D	212
4.	A	213
5.	A	213
6.	A	218
7	A	220
8.	D	222
9.	B	222
10.	D	222

True-False

1.	F	212
2.	T	213
3.	T	213-215
4.	T	216
5.	F	217
6.	T	219-220
7.	T	221
8.	T	221
9.	T	222
10.	T	222-223

Completion

1.	longbow	209
2.	*Jacquerie*	209-211
3.	nationalism	212
4.	*Decameron*	214
5.	Church and state	216-218
6.	John XXII	219
7.	University of Prague	220
8.	John Huss	221
9.	Babylonian Captivity	221
10.	*Execrabilis*	222

◆ ◆ ◆ ◆ ◆ ◆ ◆

RENAISSANCE AND DISCOVERY

COMMENTARY

Despite the turbulence of these times European life was changing. Medieval states would soon give way to their modern counterparts. The irregularity of these changes, however, would lead to serious and often long-term disputes within the emerging European state system. All of these changes will be further stimulated by the Protestant Reformation which began in 1517 and is the subject of Chapter 11.

It was in Italy during the late Middle Ages that the true outlines of Renaissance life and culture could be seen. The Italian city-states were the crossroads of Mediterranean trade and as such enjoyed a degree of urban sophistication unmatched anywhere else in Europe. Florence, Milan, Venice, Rome, and Naples were major centers of Renaissance life. Today an examination of the social and political divisions in Florence can serve as an example of the Renaissance political experience. The age was truly a period of transformation from things old and medieval to things new and modern.

In the environment of the late Middle Ages in Italy appeared the Renaissance spirit of Humanism. However it be specifically defined, Humanism was the key to Renaissance culture. Scholars today usually consider Francesco Petrarch as the founder of the new philosophy. But the Humanist spirit was not confined to philosophy, for it was the very intellectual foundation of the great cultural achievements traditionally associated with this era. New patterns of inquiry emerged as scholars went beyond the confines of Scholasticism into broader areas of study. With more materials available for them to examine antiquity and past teachings they outlined the basis of liberal studies. Their work inspired wide-ranging changes in educational traditions and ushered in a new spirit of criticism. Realism in the visual arts supported and enlarged the view Renaissance peoples had of themselves and remains a visible demonstration of their spirit. The end of the fifteenth and well into the sixteenth century witnessed the preeminence of the great masters of the High Renaissance: Leonardo da Vinci, Raphael, and Michaelangelo.

France, Spain, and England would reach a degree of centralized authority in the fifteenth century. These states, led by new, nationalistically inclined monarchies, would be in position to expand outward in what now marks the first stage of European imperialism. At the same time, and somewhat emblematic of the recent history of Germany, the Holy Roman Empire remained divided by over three hundred sources of authority. The Golden Bull of 1356 gave some semblance of centralization to Germany, but rarely had the effect of overcoming the historic divisions of this vast central European territory. This process would be further aggravated by the advent of Protestantism.

As Italy was the center of the Renaissance it also became the prey of the increasingly centralized states to the north. On the eve of the Reformation the Italian city-states already had been appropriately humbled as the center of European political, economic and social change shifted northward.

Clearly this era in which the Middle Ages ended was a time of considerable change. These permutations to the fundamental life-style of the Europeans went well beyond the changes characterized by the Renaissance, and in many ways the impact was clearly world-ranging. Combined with Europe's "discovery" of Africa, the Spanish conquest in the America's and the resulting influx of new monies into the European commercial network, this period virtually ended the Middle Ages. The effects of these so-called "discoveries" remain a part of the history and culture of these once conquered peoples—a legacy that extends at least to the end of this century.

In this era the emerging new-styled monarchs extended their control over vast areas of the non-European world and tightened their control over their own peoples. Inflation and the intellectual ferment brought on by the Humanists further contributed to this atmosphere of change. The forthcoming Protestant challenges to church authority additionally would set in motion substantial waves of change in all aspects of European life.

IDENTIFICATIONS

**CHAPTER 10
RENAISSANCE AND
DISCOVERY**

Identify each one of the following as used in the text. Refer to the text as necessary.

	Text Page
Gulf and Ghibelline	225
Cosimo de' Medici	226-227
condottieri	227
Leonardo Bruni	227
Manuel Chrysoloras	228
Christine de Pisan	229
slavery in the Renaissance	233-234
Girolamo Savonarola	235
League of Venice	235
Concordat of Bologna	236
Parliament, Estates General, Cortes	237
Louis XI	238
Tomas de Torquemada	239
Court of Star Chamber	240
Golden Bull of 1356	241
Johann Gutenberg	242
Desiderius Erasmus	243
Francisco Jimenez de Cisneros	244-245
Montezuma	248
hacienda	249
peninsulares and *creoles*	249
encomienda	249
repartimiento	249

MAP EXERCISE A

Locate or outline the boundaries of each of the following:

1. Papal States
2. Kingdom of Naples
3. Republic of Venice
4. Duchy of Milan
5. Republic of Genoa
6. Republic of Florence
7. Calabria
8. Ottoman Empire
9. Rome
10. Naples
11. Venice
12. Milan
13. Genoa
14. Florence
15. Palermo
16. Siena

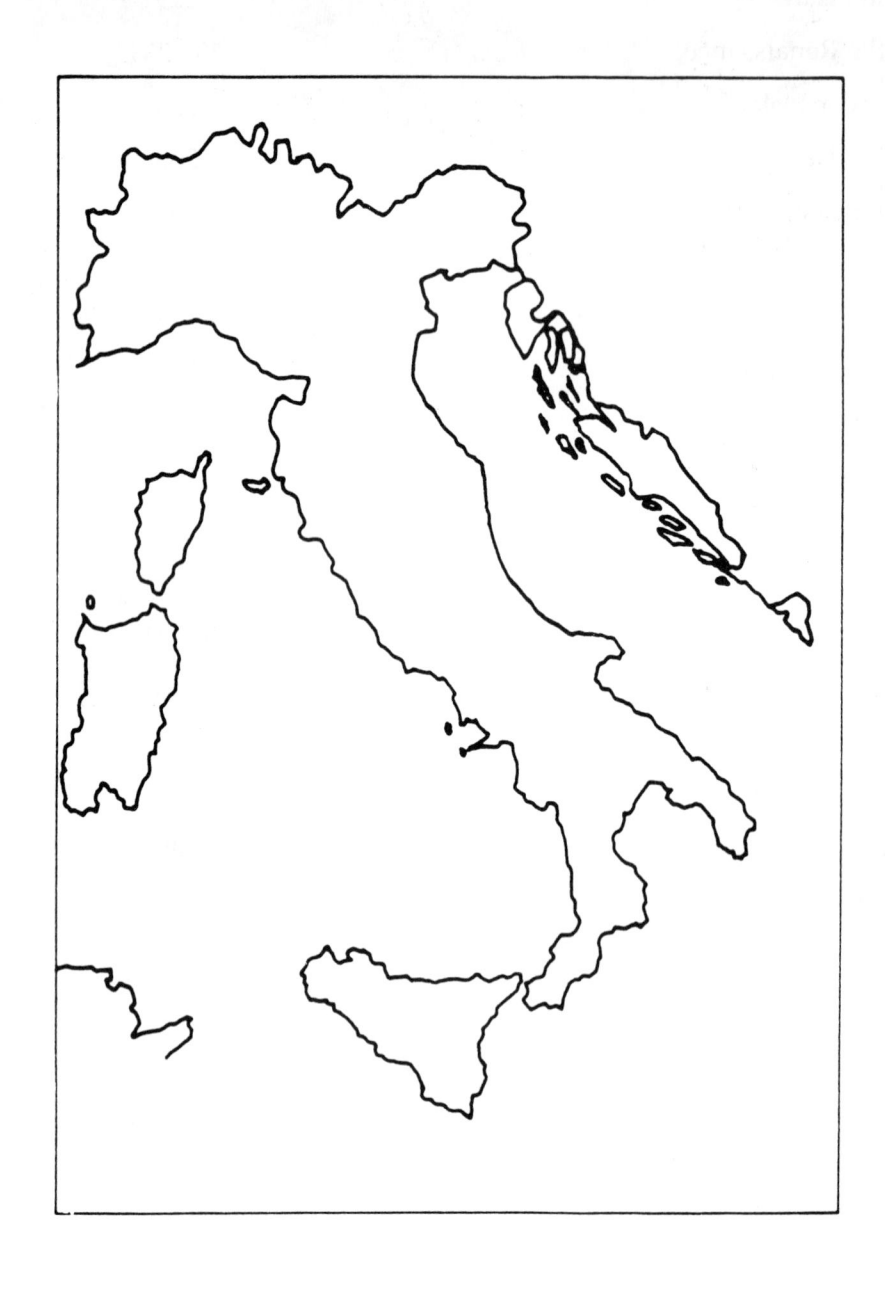

MAP EXERCISE B

On this contemporary world map, mark the major areas of European discovery and conquest by Spain, Portugal, England and France.

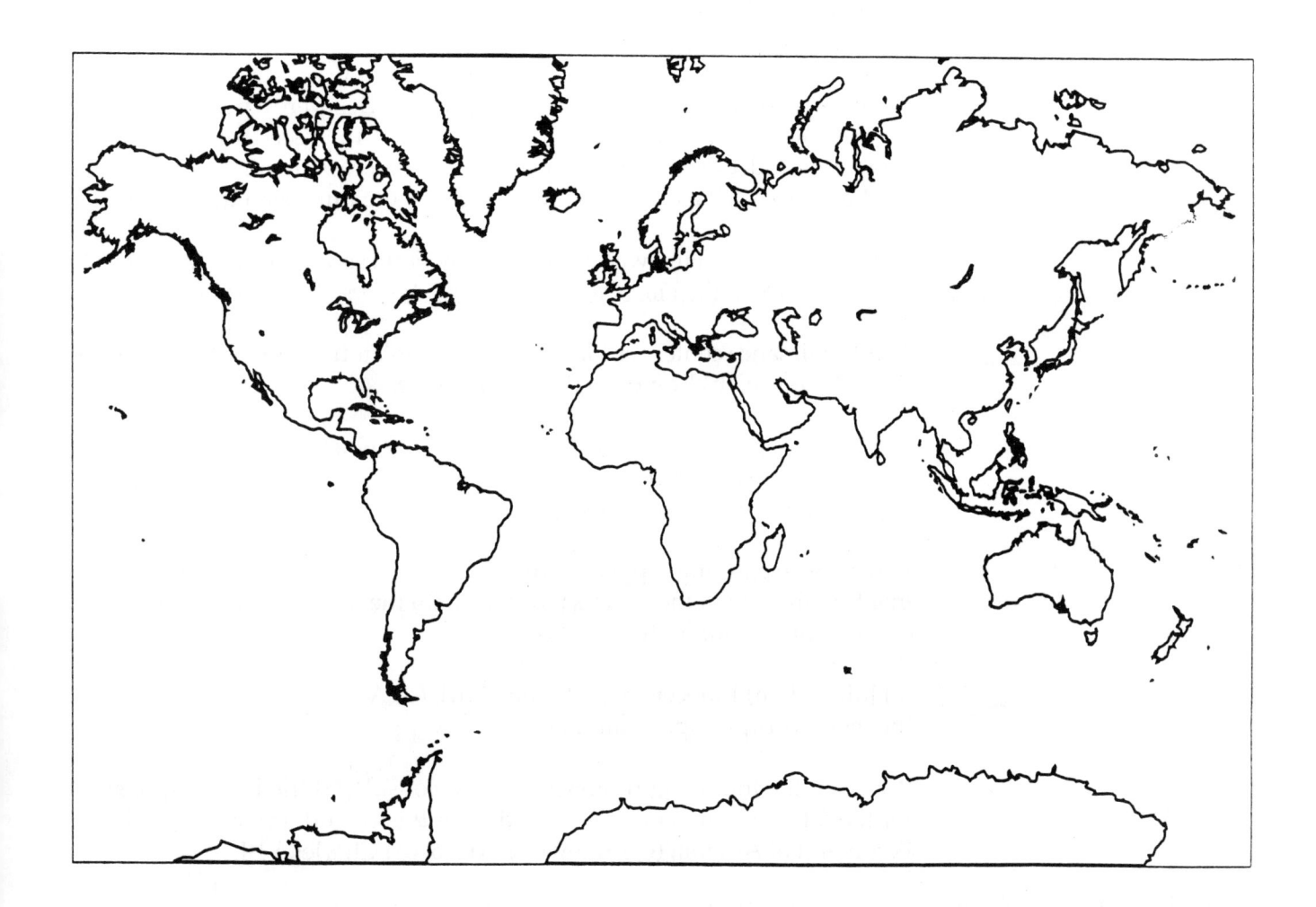

Short-Answer Exercises

Multiple-Choice

_____ 1. This entire period of the late Middle Ages is considered a period of: (a) creative breaking up, (b) decline and harvest, (c) unprecedented difficulty, (d) all of these.

_____ 2. For Europe the late fifteenth and sixteenth centuries were a period that saw: (a) the collapse of the Atlantic slave trade, (b) unprecedented territorial growth and ideological experimentation, (c) successful curtailing of ideas by the Church, (d) a continued weakening of the European trade system.

_____ 3. Which of the following was not written by Francesco Petrarch: (a) *Letters to the Ancient Dead*, (b) *Vita Nuova*, (c) *Africa*, (d) *Lives of Illustrious Men*.

_____ 4. The Renaissance center for Platonist and Neoplatonist thought was the city of: (a) Florence, (b) Rome, (c) Paris, (d) Venice.

_____ 5. The Renaissance gave a new perspective to life which is probably best evidenced in: (a) warfare, (b) music and literature, (c) painting and sculpture, (d) education and philosophy.

_____ 6. Renaissance paintings appeared three-dimensional as a result of: (a) adjustments to the size of the figures portrayed, (b) the use of shading, (c) the use of oil paints, (d) all of these.

_____ 7. (a) Julius II, (b) Innocent III, (c) John XXIII, (d) Alexander VI, is considered the most corrupt Pope of all times.

_____ 8. Which of the following figures would be considered the least responsible for the fall of the Italian city-states during this period: (a) Machiavelli, (b) Ferdinand of Aragon, (c) Ludovico il Moro, (d) Charles VIII.

_____ 9. Machiavelli's *The Prince* was dedicated to: (a) Holy Roman Emperor Charles V, (b) Lorenzo de' Medici, (c) Lorenzo the Magnificent, (d) Pope Clement VII.

_____ 10. The creation of an electoral college for the Holy Roman Empire can be found in the: (a) Imperial Council of Regency, (b) Golden Bull of 1356, (c) Assembly at Worms, (d) none of these.

True-False

_____ 1. Within the divisions of Florentine society in the Renaissance era the *popolo minuto* were viewed as the highest.

_____ 2. The goal of humanistic studies was to locate and root out evil at every level of society.

_____ 3. The father of Renaissance painting was Giotto.

_____ 4. Surprisingly, Michelangelo's famous statue of *David* is only eight feet high.

_____ 5. The *gabelle*, the *alcabala*, and the *taille* were forms of taxation levied by feudal monarchs.

_____ 6. In the fifteenth century the imperial diet was a ceremonial meal taken by several German princes publicly in the *Reichstag*.

_____ 7. Johann Reuchlin invented the printing press.

_____ 8. Study of original versions of early Christian literature, a call for simple piety, and a disciplined study of the Bible are virtues said to have been encouraged by Desiderius Erasmus.

_____ 9. The 1516 work *Utopia* by Thomas More suggested that a distinct division of social classes and personal property would make for an ideal society.

_____ 10. The Aztecs believed that the gods must literally be fed with human bodies to guarantee continuing sunshine and soil fertility.

Completion

1. The _____ Revolt was the great uprising of the poor in Florence.

2. The unification of Spain was effected by the marriage in 1469 of Isabella of _____ to Ferdinand of _____ .

3. The text notes _____ as one of the most authoritative writers on the concept of Humanism during the Renaissance era.

4. The works of _____ and _____ are said to form the basis of the Italian vernacular language.

5. _____ was an influential book which stressed the importance of integrating knowledge of language and history with other skills while calling for good manners and high moral character.

6. The Donation of Constantine was fraudulent document which had supported Church claims to vast territories in Italy, but was exposed in the fifteenth century by the humanist scholar _____ .

7. _____ was a fresco portraying the great minds of Western philosophy.

8. The most famous of the northern Christian Humanist of this era was _____.

9. _____ was Europe's foremost authority on Jewish learning before his death in 1522.

10. The late fifteenth and sixteenth century saw the maturation of the economic concept of _____.

FOR FURTHER CONSIDERATION

1. Give a complete definition of Humanism. Describe key Humanistic ideas within the context of the Renaissance. What is the debate over Jacob Burckhart's nineteenth century description of this era?

2. How did the Humanist experience develop within Renaissance politics? Additionally, discuss the influence of the Humanistic spirit on the medieval concepts of education. Give specific examples.

3. Why did Italy attract the European rulers at the end of the fifteenth century? How was it that the great Italian city-states could not stand against the northern invaders? What new rivalries were created by these invasions?

4. Discuss this early phase in the rise of national monarchies from the perspective of administrative bureaucracies, standing armies, and taxation.

5. Mindful of this quincentenary era (1492-1992) of Columbus' landing in the Americas, describe the initial contact between the Europeans and the Amer-Indians they encountered. Is there a pattern to these encounters? Over the centuries since that time, what has been the historic view of Europe's discovery of the "New World?"

Answers

Multiple-Choice

		Text Page
1.	A	224
2.	B	224-225
3.	B	228
4.	A	229-231
5.	C	232
6.	D	232
7.	D	235
8.	A	235
9.	B	236
10.	B	241

True-False

1.	F	226
2.	F	229
3.	T	232
4.	F	233
5.	T	238
6.	F	241
7.	F	242
8.	T	243
9.	F	244
10.	T	248

Completion

1.	Ciompi Revolt	226
2.	Dante Alighieri/ Francesco Petrarch	229
3.	*The Book of the Courtier*	229
4.	Lorenzo Valla	231
5.	*The School of Athens*	233
6.	Estates General	237
7.	Castile/Aragon	238-239
8.	Desiderius Erasmus	243
9.	Johann Reuchlin	244
10.	capitalism	250

◆ ◆ ◆ ◆ ◆ ◆ ◆

FOR FURTHER CONSIDERATION OF THE DOCUMENTS

Each of the following questions is designed to help you reach a better understanding of the original documents presented in the last five chapters of the text. Feel free to use the page numbers provided to refer back to the document as necessary. The value of a primary historical source should not be underestimated; it helps us understand the nature of the era in which it was written.

Attila (p. 137)
1. What in this document suggest that heads of state, such as Attila, should live on a scale above ordinary people? Why, even in modern democracies, are leading political figures accorded such respect?

English Restraints on King John (p. 177)
2. The seven concept listed in this excerpt from the Magna Carta outline basic principles that have persisted into the modern legal and political systems of the West. List each of these categories and place them in the context of modern legal/political practice.

Students at the University of Paris (p. 200)
3. From this reading, comment on cultural diversity, intolerance, racism as factors in modern student life? How is college/university life affected by these attitudes? Are there problems on your campus? What can you suggest as the best way to resolve cultural and racial differences on any campus?

Ravages of the Black Death (p. 214)
4. Could Boccaccio's description of problems relating to the plague be applied to the modern pestilence of AIDS? Write a modern description in the pattern outlined in the *Decameron*?

Pico Della Mirandola on the Renaissance Image of Man (p. 230)
5. What does he mean by "Thou shalt have the power to degenerate into the lower forms of life, which are brutish?"

From Chapters 6-10

Chapter 11

The Age of Reformation

Commentary

What is historically presented as the Reformation is a period of European transformation rooted in the sixteenth and early seventeenth centuries. This Protestant movement challenged the Roman Catholic Church's powerful position and set in motion substantial waves of change in all aspects of European life.

For almost two centuries before Martin Luther's challenge to church authority, Scholastics and Humanists had been studying the mysteries of church teaching. Their works, appearing before an ever-widening reading audience in Europe, had a great impact. The weakness of the church in the late Middle Ages was demonstrated through corrupt popes, schisms, and controversial doctrinal issues left unresolved. As the sixteenth century began, the European world was in a condition and mood that would more readily than ever be receptive to a sweeping assault upon church tradition. In 1517 Luther was to place the final straw upon the back of the medieval church camel.

An Augustinian priest, Martin Luther was by 1512 well-schooled in theology and like many of his age troubled by many aspects of that theology. His concept of justification by faith alone came from his introspection, prayer, and a thorough knowledge of Scripture. Initially his challenge on the issue of indulgences centered on the particular emphasis given by the notorious preacher John Tetzel. Luther's 95 theses argued that these indulgences as preached in nearby Saxony were beyond the established tradition. By 1520 he was well past the issue of indulgences and had clearly crossed paths already condemned by the church council a century before at Constance. The almost simultaneous controversy over the election of a Holy Roman Emperor in 1519 drew attention away from Luther and allowed Protestantism to gain an entrenched position within the empire. Not willing to reverse his position and recant his views, Luther was condemned by the Imperial Diet at Worms in 1521. Problems with the French in the west and the Turks in the east prevented the new Emperor Charles V from turning full attention to what was the beginning of the Reformation.

Luther's struggle with church authority was immediately echoed in several areas of the empire. It appeared that once loosened church authority would be widely challenged; and it was! Other reformers were soon ranging across theology to prove their particular interpretations of Scripture over that of Rome. Secular rulers anxious to gain advantage in this turn of events were soon involved in doctrinal disputes that spilled over onto the battlefield.

Both the second half of the sixteenth century and the entire Protestant scene were dominated by the religious reformer of Geneva, John Calvin. By 1555 Calvin was entrenched with his followers in control of that Swiss city-state and his doctrines were spreading throughout Europe. Geneva had become a center for religious refugees from all over Europe.

Against this back drop of the struggle between conflicting religious ideologies one finds many important and interesting responses. Among these responses is nationalism. A most powerful ideology destined to have profound impact on Western history to our time. The Reformation impacted in the New World as well and stimulated competition between the European states throughout the Americas.

The Reformation in England was not simply the result of a doctrinal dispute but rather was related to the complicated personality and succession problem of Henry VIII. From 1527 through the Act of Supremacy in 1534, and through the dissolutions of the monasteries beginning in 1536, England moved into the Protestant fold. Henry VIII's wives were as much a difficulty as his stormy relationships with a series of ministers and legates of the Church. Surprisingly, Henry's religious views remained conservatively Catholic throughout his reign. When Henry died, his successor, the ten-year-old boy Edward VI, would never truly reign but did preside over a country moving headlong into Protestantism. To add to the internal confusion within England, Edward's death at age sixteen brought his most Catholic half-sister Mary to power. In the five years before her death, Mary attempted to restore Catholicism. Her efforts passed with her as her Protestant half-sister Elizabeth's reign of forty-five years confirmed Protestantism in England.

Even before 1517, however, the Roman Church had attempted to carry out limited reforms. These were under such strict papal supervision that little came of the attempts as Renaissance popes jealously guarded their primacy. After 1517, and by encouraging the activities of newly formed Counter Reformation religious orders and eventually through the workings of a major church council, the Catholic Church was able to offset much of the initial Protestant success. European Christians throughout this century were indeed caught in the middle of powerful religious ideologies. which in themselves were altering the course of the Western heritage.

All the debate over religion in the sixteenth century had a lasting effect upon European life. Although one can argue, and persuasively, that the advent of Protestantism constituted only a new conservatism, one which would replace that of the medieval period, it seems unquestionable that changes at every level of European life followed in the wake of the religious revolution. Protestants appear to have rejected the universalism of the church for modern and more secular individualism and in doing so to have affected the nature of Western life ever since. The doctrines espoused in this religious upheaval caused fundamental changes in the Western view of life, in the development of society, in marriage patterns, religious life, education, and in the position of women in society.

This beginning of more than one hundred years of religiously inspired bloodshed represented an organized violence that further transformed the character of European life. Involved in this transformation were the concepts of capitalism and nationalism. In these troubled times secular power continued to grow as universal religious authority ebbed. Wars were great stimuli to the growth of government, even as they are in modern times. And these effects of the Protestant Reformation would spread throughout Europe and to the New World.

Identifications

Identify each one of the following as used in the text. Refer to the text as necessary.

	Text Page
Thomas à Kempis	255
indulgences	257-258
Archbishop Albrecht	258-259
Diet of Worms (May 1521)	261
Battle of Mohacs	261
Philip of Hesse	263
Anabaptism	263
Schleitheim Confession	264
Antitrinitarians	264
John Calvin	265-266
Europe's only "free" city	266
Statutes of Provisors and *Praemunire*	267
William Tyndale	267
Leviticus 18:16, 20:21	267
Six Articles of 1539	268
Catherine Parr	269
Book of Common Prayer	269
cuius regio, eius religio	271
Fifth Lateran Council	271
Ursulines	272
Oratorians	272
Spiritual Exercises	272
"Black Legend"	274
Philip Melanchthon	276
birth control practices of this era	279

MAP EXERCISE A

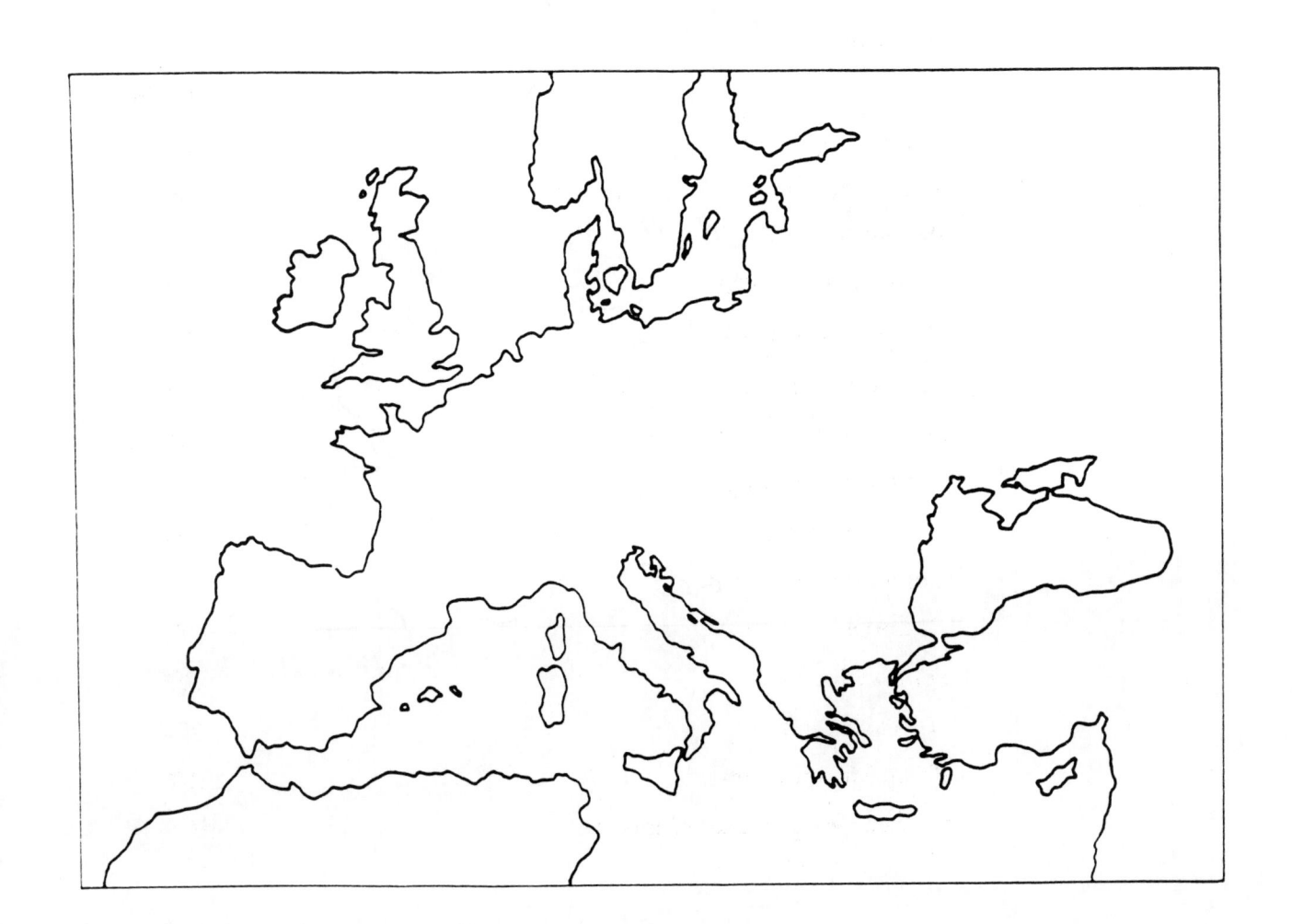

Outline/locate each of the following on the accompanying map:

1. England and Scotland
2. Sweden
3. Spain (and European territory)
4. Holy Roman Empire
5. Denmark
6. Netherlands
7. Russia
8. France
9. Portugal
10. Atlantic Ocean
11. North Sea
12. Black Sea
13. Baltic Sea
14. Adriatic Sea
15. London
16. Constance
17. Wittenberg
18. Worms
19. Geneva
20. Trent
21. Cambridge
22. Augsburg
23. Paris
24. Madrid

Map Exercise B

On this map of the British Isles mark the boundaries of England, Ireland, Scotland and Wales. Locate the cities of London, Dublin, Edinburgh and Cardiff. Locate the following bodies of water: Thames River, Dublin Bay, Firth of Forth and the Bristol Channel. Mark also the Irish Sea, North Sea and the Strait of Dover.

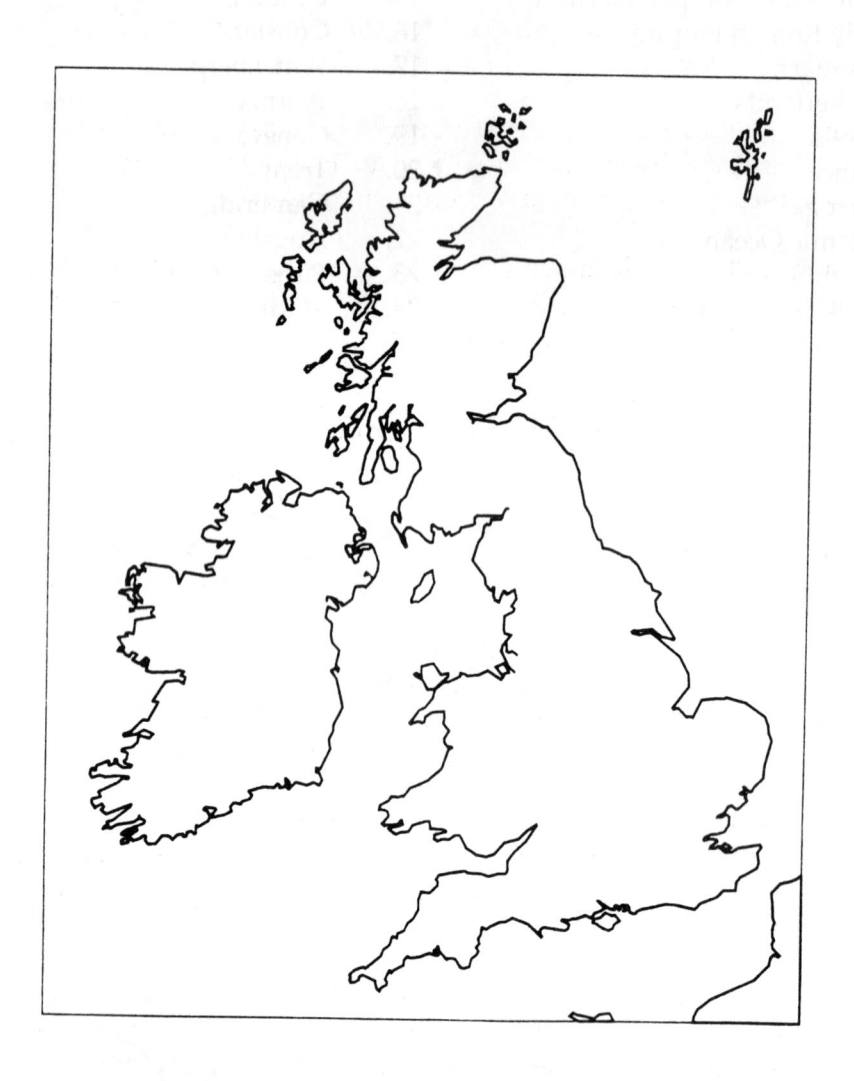

Short-Answer Exercises

Multiple-Choice

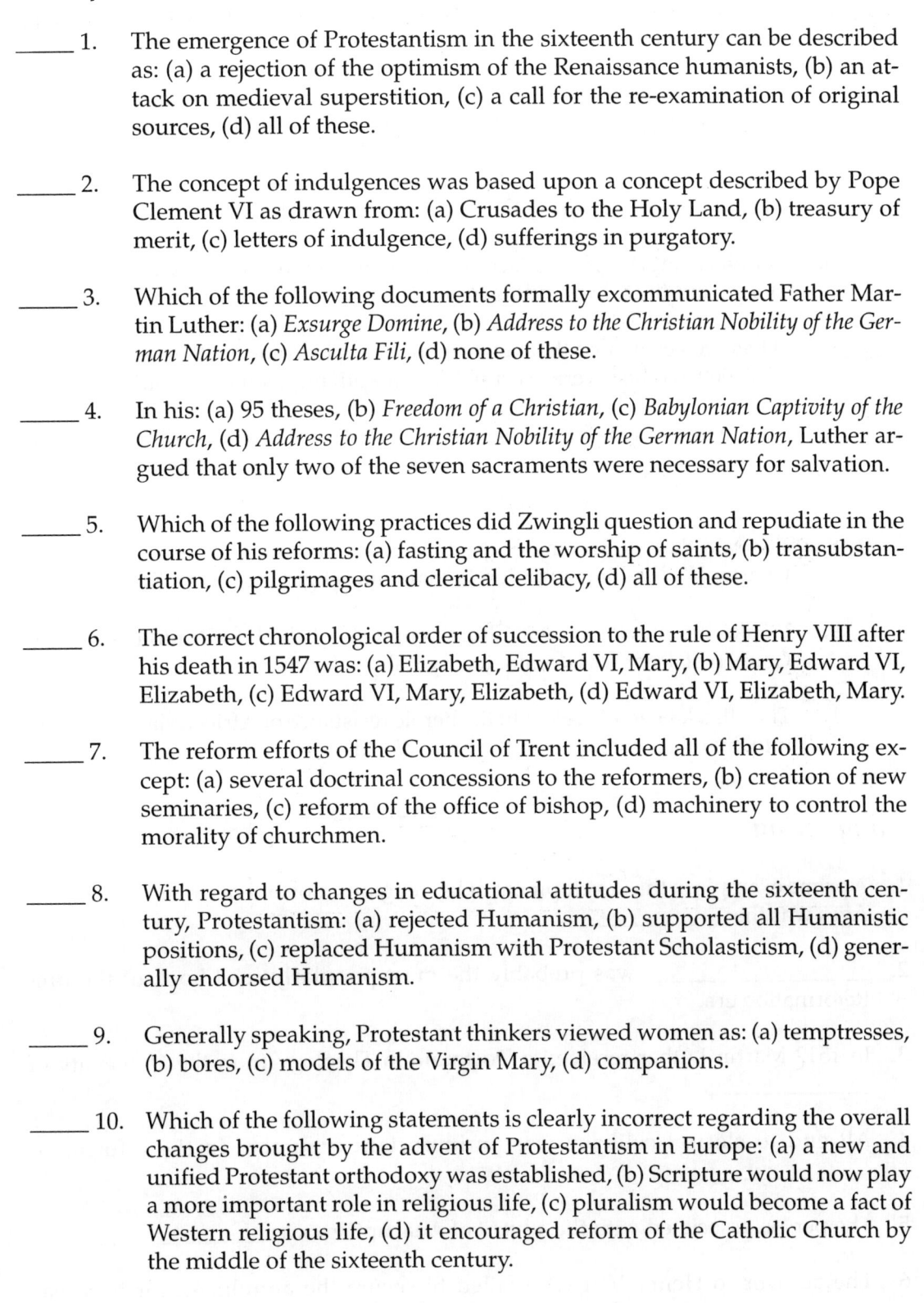

_____ 1. The emergence of Protestantism in the sixteenth century can be described as: (a) a rejection of the optimism of the Renaissance humanists, (b) an attack on medieval superstition, (c) a call for the re-examination of original sources, (d) all of these.

_____ 2. The concept of indulgences was based upon a concept described by Pope Clement VI as drawn from: (a) Crusades to the Holy Land, (b) treasury of merit, (c) letters of indulgence, (d) sufferings in purgatory.

_____ 3. Which of the following documents formally excommunicated Father Martin Luther: (a) *Exsurge Domine*, (b) *Address to the Christian Nobility of the German Nation*, (c) *Asculta Fili*, (d) none of these.

_____ 4. In his: (a) 95 theses, (b) *Freedom of a Christian*, (c) *Babylonian Captivity of the Church*, (d) *Address to the Christian Nobility of the German Nation*, Luther argued that only two of the seven sacraments were necessary for salvation.

_____ 5. Which of the following practices did Zwingli question and repudiate in the course of his reforms: (a) fasting and the worship of saints, (b) transubstantiation, (c) pilgrimages and clerical celibacy, (d) all of these.

_____ 6. The correct chronological order of succession to the rule of Henry VIII after his death in 1547 was: (a) Elizabeth, Edward VI, Mary, (b) Mary, Edward VI, Elizabeth, (c) Edward VI, Mary, Elizabeth, (d) Edward VI, Elizabeth, Mary.

_____ 7. The reform efforts of the Council of Trent included all of the following except: (a) several doctrinal concessions to the reformers, (b) creation of new seminaries, (c) reform of the office of bishop, (d) machinery to control the morality of churchmen.

_____ 8. With regard to changes in educational attitudes during the sixteenth century, Protestantism: (a) rejected Humanism, (b) supported all Humanistic positions, (c) replaced Humanism with Protestant Scholasticism, (d) generally endorsed Humanism.

_____ 9. Generally speaking, Protestant thinkers viewed women as: (a) temptresses, (b) bores, (c) models of the Virgin Mary, (d) companions.

_____ 10. Which of the following statements is clearly incorrect regarding the overall changes brought by the advent of Protestantism in Europe: (a) a new and unified Protestant orthodoxy was established, (b) Scripture would now play a more important role in religious life, (c) pluralism would become a fact of Western religious life, (d) it encouraged reform of the Catholic Church by the middle of the sixteenth century.

True-False

_____ 1. The Reformation started in Germany and Switzerland.

_____ 2. Popular on the eve of the Reformation lay religious movements generally shared a common goal of religious simplicity and apostolic poverty.

_____ 3. Turkish attacks in the Eastern Empire and several wars against France in Italy managed to distract Charles V as the Protestant Reformation began in earnest.

_____ 4. Martin Luther supported the German Peasants' Revolt of 1524-25.

_____ 5. Ulrich Zwingli opposed each of the following: mercenary service, celibate clergy, and the sale of indulgences.

_____ 6. It has been estimated that between the years 1525 and 1618 between 100,000 - 500,000 women were executed for rebaptizing themselves as adults.

_____ 7. "If a man takes his brother's wife, they shall be without children," appears in Leviticus 20, and was a serious admonition against Henry VIII's first marriage.

_____ 8. It is said that the signing of the 1552 Peace of Passau gained the Emperor Charles V's life-long ambition to maintain religious unity in Europe.

_____ 9. Unlike the previous great Church councils of the later Middle Ages, the Council of Trent was dominated by Italian clerics.

_____ 10. The "Black Legend" refers to the heroic resistance of African slaves brought into Spain's possessions in the New World.

Completion

1. A prime example in the development of lay religious movements in the late Middle Ages was the _____.

2. _____ was probably the most popularly read book of the pre-Reformation era.

3. In 1512 Martin Luther received a Doctorate in Theology from the University of _____.

4. All end to clerical celibacy was an important argument in the reforms of _____.

5. The person associated with the advent of Anabaptism was _____.

6. The advisor to Henry VIII who failed to secure the annulment for him was _____.

7. The official document that made the king/queen of England head of the church there was _____.

8. The Council of _____ was a most important effort in the Church's Counter-Reformation.

9. Generally Protestant reforms had the effect of reducing the medieval concept of the distinction between the clergy and the _____.

10. Protestant teachings had a definite effect upon the role of _____ in society.

FOR FURTHER CONSIDERATION

1. Assess religious attitudes in Europe before Luther. Were these views related to the weakness of the papacy and the church organization at the time or were other factors involved? Explain your answer fully.

2. Describe Calvin's life and the times through which he lived. How would you assess his role as ruler of Geneva? What has been the impact of Calvin's teachings in Europe? In America?

3. Protestant radicalism was well entrenched by the end of the sixteenth century despite efforts by Catholics and other Protestant denominations to stop the spread. Describe several of these radical religious philosophies. What effect, if any, did they have on the Reformation?

4. How would you describe the overall impact of the Protestant Reformation upon sixteenth-century Europe? How did the rise of Protestantism permanently alter the course of Western civilization?

5. Having studied in the last several chapters the doctrines of the Roman Catholic Church as well as those of the various Protestant reformers, could you envision the possibility that a religious settlement could be reached in our time by which the Christian faith would again be one? Support your answer both from a historical perspective and through contemporary analysis.

Answers

Multiple-Choice

		Text Page
1.	D	252-253
2.	B	257
3.	C	261
4.	D	261
5.	D	263
6.	C	269
7.	A	274
8.	D	277
9.	D	277
10.	A	280

True-False

1.	T	253
2.	T	255
3.	T	261
4.	F	261-262
5.	T	262-263
6.	F	264
7.	T	267
8.	F	270
9.	T	273
10.	F	274

Completion

1.	Modern Devotion/ Brothers of the Common Life	255
2.	*Imitation of Christ*	255
3.	Wittenberg	257
4.	Ulrich Zwingli	262
5.	Conrad Grebel	263
6.	Cardinal Wolsey	268
7.	Act of Supremacy	268
8.	Trent	272-274
9.	laity/ordinary persons	276
10.	women	277-278

◆ ◆ ◆ ◆ ◆ ◆ ◆

Chapter 12

THE AGE OF RELIGIOUS WARS

COMMENTARY

From the time of Luther's death in 1546 until the middle of the seventeenth century, European life was almost entirely dominated by religiously, and often politically, inspired violence. Warfare in Germany introduced levels of human destruction higher than had previously been experienced, while in England a government was toppled in violence and a king was beheaded by his people. Roman Catholics on the one hand and the more factious Protestants on the other engaged in almost a century of slaughter before accommodating each other as fellow Christians.

The struggle in France between Protestant Huguenots and Catholics continued for half a century. Intermittent truces only allowed the respective factions to regain their strength for the following round of killing. Incidents such as the St. Bartholomew's Day Massacre in 1572, in which 20,000 Protestants were slaughtered, aggravated the situation beyond the norm. Although never dominant in numbers, Huguenots had considerable influence in several important urban locations and soon represented nearly 40 percent of the French nobility. As elsewhere in Europe the acceptance of Protestant beliefs created political advantages for those already predisposed to challenge the monarchy. Resistance to Catholic-monarchial-aristocratic rule was becoming an important tenet with Protestant groups struggling for their beliefs. By 1598 the French had reached a settlement. The Edict of Nantes was at best a compromise and remained an uneasy symbol of the political and religious reality. This document gave religious freedoms to the minority Huguenots, complete with assurances of their control over certain "Protestant" cities. It asked all concerned to simply forget the struggles "as if it were something which had never occurred." Henry IV (Henry of Navarre), himself an uncertain "Catholic," had ended the struggle, but the seeds for its continuance had not been plowed under very deeply. It should be noted that though shortened by assassination, Henry's reign set in motion a process that would create French absolutism under his grandson Louis XIV.

The unparalleled wealth of Spain in the sixteenth century, which was drawn from its American empire, gave that country enormous political leverage within its borders and ultimately in European affairs. The ascetic Philip II, who controlled Spain for the last forty years of that century and straitjacketed the Spanish clergy, nobility, and peasantry, forged Spain's all-powerful position during this era. The defeat of the Turkish fleet at Lepanto in 1571 gave Spain even greater prestige and added to her authority in European affairs. However, Spain was not to have her way in all things. Bloodied by the English victory over the "Invincible" Armada and his failure to subdue Protestantism and nationalism in the Netherlands, Philip's strength was sapped. As a result, Spain's position in international affairs would wane in the next century.

In England the Protestant - Catholic conflict involved less warfare but more bitterness. The comparatively brief reigns of Edward VI and Mary Tudor which followed that of their father Henry VIII, left much confusion and doubt among ordinary citizens. The reign of yet another of Henry's children, Elizabeth I, temporarily resolved the religious debate there. An intelligently moderate religious settlement early in her reign set the stage for the growing international prestige enjoyed by Elizabethan England. The execution of Mary, Queen of Scots early in 1587 heightened Catholic concerns for the future of Catholicism in England; but the defeat of the Spanish Armada the next year was a sure sign of Elizabeth's and England's success in this era. Although the next century would belong to France, England's emergence as a world power, thanks to good Queen Bess, was at hand.

For Germany, this era, which had opened with the religious compromise of Augsburg (1555) was to prove disastrous for future unification. In this, the original center of the Reformation, Lutherans and Catholics, after some bloodletting, had come to tolerate each other. But neither Lutherans nor Catholics had any use for what they considered to be more radical religious approaches, especially those deriving from the teachings of John Calvin. By the early seventeenth century and after religious compromises had been worked out in England and France, the temporary compromise in Germany collapsed. The resulting free-for-all, known historically as the Thirty Years' War (1618-1648), went through four distinguishable phases and remains a rich example of human malevolence. The conflict effectively consumed much of Europe's energies until it was seemingly resolved in the international settlement of Westphalia. Hence, after 1648, though the peoples of central Europe would remain deeply divided, religion would no longer be a primary factor in international conflict as it had been since the Reformation began.

IDENTIFICATIONS

Identify each one of the following as used in the text. Refer to the text as necessary.

	Text Page
presbyters	283
politiques	283
Besançon Hugues	284
Gaspard de Coligny	285
Peace of St. Germain-en-Laye	286
The Escorial	290
Don John	291
William of Orange	291-292
Spanish Fury	293
Duke of Alençon	293
"Marian Exiles"	294
Sir William Cecil	294-295
Duke of Medina-Sidonia	297
Frederick III of the Palatinate	298
Letter of Majesty	301
"Defenestration at Prague"	301
Albrecht of Wallenstein	301
Gustavus Adolphus	301

Map Exercise A

Outline/locate each of the following areas on the accompanying map:

1. Name and trace four major rivers
2. English Channel
3. Name and locate six European seas
4. Major Catholic areas or countries
5. Major Anglican areas or countries
6. Major Calvinist areas or countries
7. Major Lutheran areas or countries

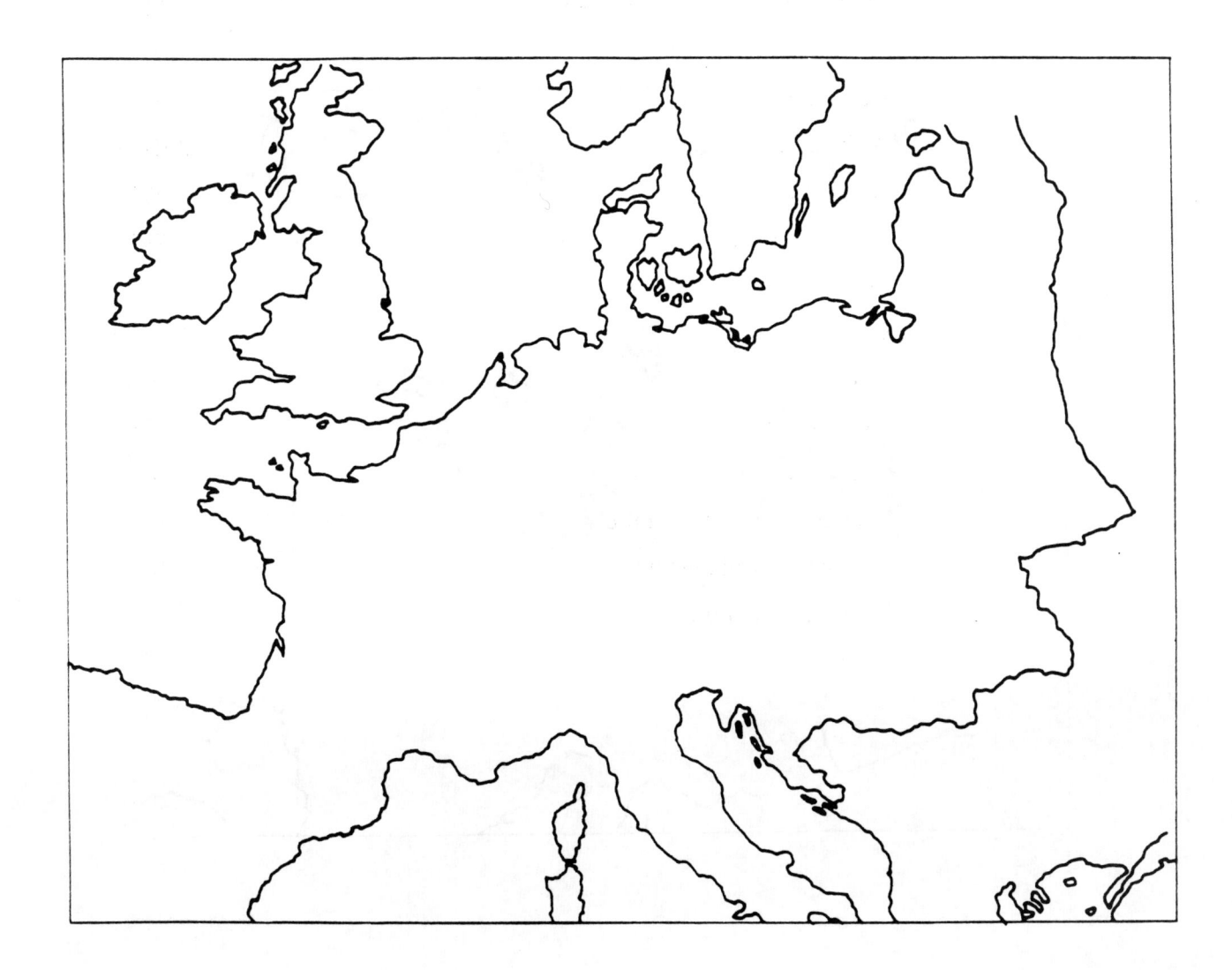

Chapter 12
The Age of Religious Wars

Map Exercise B

Utilizing the accompanying map of North Central Europe at the time of the Thirty Years War, mark or outline each of the following places/areas.

- Bavaria
- Bohemia
- Brandenburg
- Luxembourg
- Netherlands
- Palatinate
- Pomerania
- Prague
- Saxony
- Swiss Confederation
- Warsaw
- Westphalia
- White Mountain
- Wurtemberg

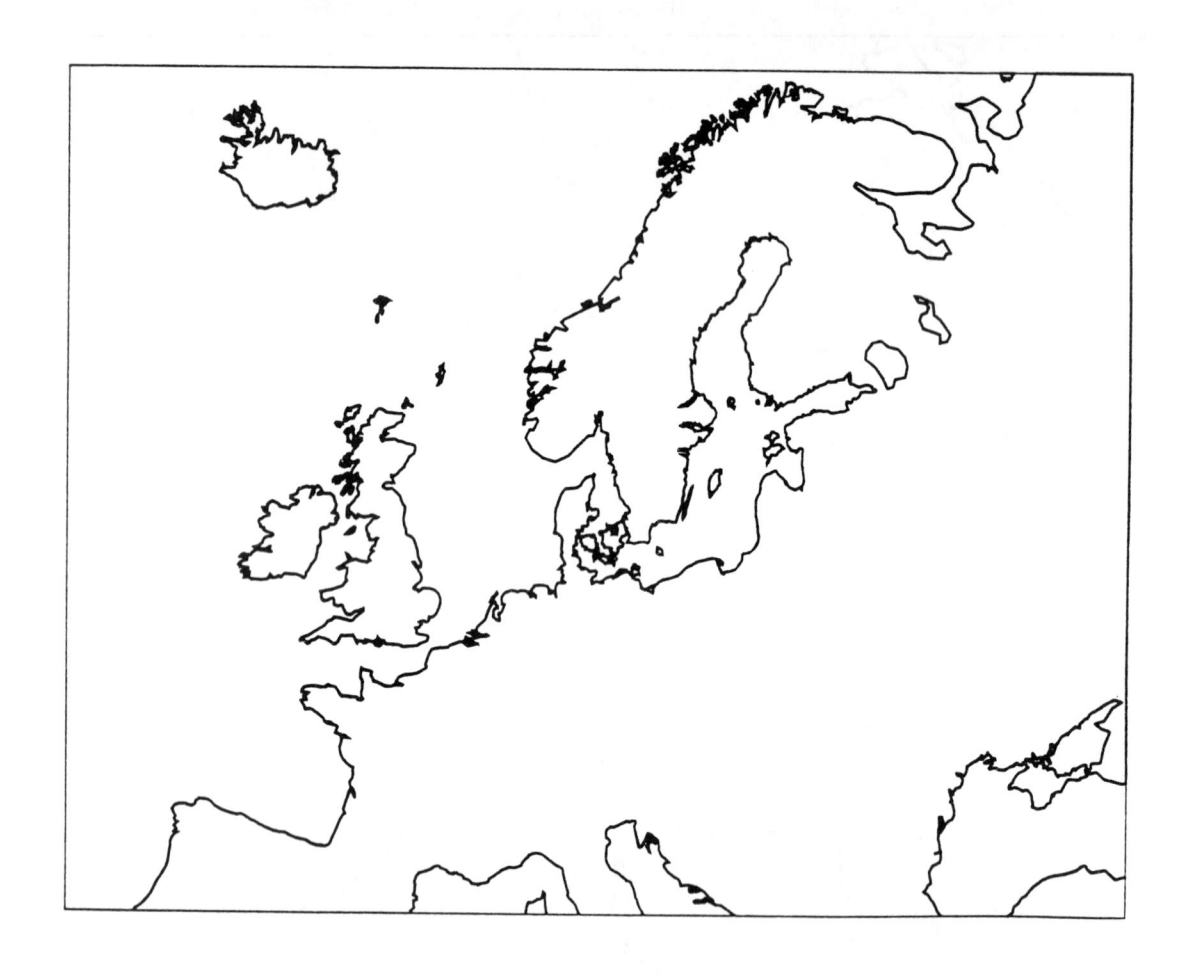

Short-Answer Exercises

Multiple-Choice

_____ 1. Which of the following is the most accurate statement about the Counter-Reformation during this era? (a) the Church emerged with an organizational structure emphasizing absolute obedience to the person at the top, (b) Catholics were permitted by the Church to convert to Lutheranism under the Augsburg Settlement, (c) the Roman Church adopted a presbyterian organization structure, (d) none of these.

_____ 2. Huguenotism, or French Calvinism, was normally supported by: (a) a majority of the population, (b) mainly the lower classes, (c) almost all the French nobility, (d) none of these.

_____ 3. Which of the following was not a work supporting the Protestant concept of defense? (a) Peace of Augsburg, (b) *Blast of the Trumpet Against the Terrible Regiment of Women*, (c) *On the Right of Magistrates over Their Subjects*, (d) *Defense of Liberty Against Tyrants*.

_____ 4. The phrase, "Paris is worth a mass," is attributed to: (a) Catherine de Médici, (b) Gaspard de Coligny, (c) Henry of Navarre, (d) Henry III.

_____ 5. In the 1560s: (a) William of Orange, (b) Duke of Alba, (c) Cardinal Granvelle, (d) Don John of Austria, brutally suppressed a Protestant uprising in the Netherlands.

_____ 6. Compared with her half-sister and successor Elizabeth, Mary I's repression of Protestantism in England is considered to be: (a) about the same, (b) more selective, (c) greater by far, (d) a model of forbearance.

_____ 7. The Elizabethan religious settlement between Protestants and Catholics that created the Anglican Church can be described as: (a) an example of Elizabeth's political ability, (b) a political-religious compromise, (c) a victory of moderate Protestantism, (d) all of these.

_____ 8. From Elizabeth I's point of view the dilemma caused by Mary, Queen of Scots was especially that she was (a) Catholic, (b) able to make a superior claim to the English throne, (c) personally jealous of Elizabeth, (d) more attractive than Elizabeth.

_____ 9. The invading fleet of the Spanish Armada was composed of approximately: (a) 75 ships, (b) 130 ships, (c) 180 ships, (d) 230 ships.

_____ 10. (a) Peace of Prague, (b) Peace of Augsburg, (c) Peace of Westphalia, (d) Edict of Restitution, formally ended the Thirty Years' War.

True-False

_____ 1. When one considers the 1555 Peace of Augsburg, it is important to note that non-Lutheran Protestants had not been included in the *cuius regio, eius religio* solution.

_____ 2. The great seventeenth century Dutch artist Rembrandt van Rijn was a devout Roman Catholic.

_____ 3. Among the three families struggling to gain control of the French monarchy after the accidental death of Henry II, the Guises were Catholic reactionaries.

_____ 4. Both Henry III and Henry IV of France were assassinated as a result of bitter religious feelings in France.

_____ 5. Since both were staunch Catholic leaders, the marriage of Philip of Spain and Mary I of England was popularly supported in both countries.

_____ 6. Spain's European influence was only set back temporarily with the defeat of the Spanish Armada.

_____ 7. An important cause of the Thirty Years' War was the fear of a German unification under a Catholic emperor.

_____ 8. On the eve of the Thirty Years' War Bavaria and the Palatinate agreed to settle their religious differences.

_____ 9. The 1629 Edict of Restitution was a dramatic milestone in the reconciliation of Calvinists with Lutherans and Catholics.

_____ 10. Spain's spectacular victories against France in the period after 1648 led to the Treaty of the Pyrenees.

Completion

1. _____ was the man who ascended the French throne in 1589.

2. The _____ formally sanctioned minority religious rights within predominately Catholic France.

3. The naval battle of _____ temporarily gave Spain control of the Mediterranean.

4. The 1572 St. Bartholomew's Day Massacre in France appears to have convinced _____ that Calvinism would be the best religious creed for the people of the Netherlands.

5. In 1553 Mary I's right to the English throne was challenged by _____.

6. The English separatists who wanted absolutely no outside interference with their religious groups were the _____.

7. _____ was the leader of the Reformation in Scotland.

8. While Mary, Queen of Scots was held under house arrest she was implicated in plots against Elizabeth I seemingly sponsored by _____ .

9. The most important center for Calvinism outside of Geneva was the German city of _____.

10. The military genius of _____ helped _____ champion the Protestant cause during the Thirty Years' War.

For Further Consideration

1. In reviewing the study of the Reformation what would you describe as the most central teachings of the Catholics, the Lutherans, and the Calvinists?

2. Compare and contrast the religious compromises worked out in the Peace of Augsburg in Germany, the Edict of Nantes in France, and the Elizabethan religious settlement in England

3. How did the concept of Protestant resistance theory reflect Protestant teachings? Would you resist serious pressure to submit or convert to a new religion? If not, Why? Explain your position fully.

4. Who was Mary Queen of Scots? Trace her life, her political and religious positions, and the circumstances of her death.

5. List in detail the terms of the Treaty of Westphalia. In your opinion which of these terms appears to have had a lasting effect on the peoples of Europe?

Answers

Multiple-Choice

		Text Page
1.	A	283
2.	D	285
3.	A	288
4.	C	289
5.	B	292
6.	C	295
7.	D	295
8.	B	296
9.	B	297
10.	C	303

True-False

1.	T	283
2.	F	283
3.	T	285
4.	T	289
5.	F	294
6.	F	297
7.	F	298
8.	F	299
9.	F	301
10.	F	303

Completion

1.	Henry of Navarre/Henry IV	289
2.	Edict of Nantes	289
3.	Lepanto	291
4.	William of Orange	292
5.	Lady Jane Grey	294
6.	Congregationalists	295
7.	John Knox	296
8.	Spain	296
9.	Heidelberg	298
10.	Gustavus Adolphus/Sweden	301

◆ ◆ ◆ ◆ ◆ ◆ ◆

Chapter 13

PATHS TO CONSTITUTIONALISM AND ABSOLUTISM: ENGLAND AND FRANCE IN THE SEVENTEENTH CENTURY

COMMENTARY

The constitutional crisis in England that followed Elizabeth's reign and continued until the end of the seventeenth century had a lasting impact on Western political life. This crisis was the result of long-developing conflict between the crown and commons. This struggle cost Charles I his head, and in the end Parliament emerged the victor. Parliamentary success was due in part to the uncompromising nature of both James I and his son Charles I. Their resolute attempts to hold onto the royal prerogatives against all political and religious opposition was an ominous factor in their defeat. During the civil war of the 1640s, Charles I was not able to resolve the conflict, and his authority slipped away. As has so often occurred in modern times, a strong man with the backing of the military reinstated executive authority, though under a different title. With the death of this man—Oliver Cromwell—in 1658 the situation went full circle. Charles I's son, Charles II, ascended the bloodstained throne with Parliamentary sanction and initiated what is referred to as the Stuart Restoration. In time, however, what had appeared under Charles II as a resolution of England's troubles worsened when his brother James II confirmed the family's Catholic sympathies. Parliament quickly dispatched James II and requested his son-in-law and daughter, William of Orange [Netherlands] and Mary, to be the sovereigns of England. From a relatively docile position under Elizabeth, the House of Commons, by the time of the Glorious Revolution, had been responsible for and directly involved in the ascendancy of three English rulers: Oliver Cromwell, Charles II, and William and Mary.

By comparison this was not a period of political transition for France, at least not in the ordinary sense. Rather, by the late seventeenth century the French monarchy had achieved its goal of centuries past: absolute control of the state and the French people. This success came as a result of the self-serving reform interests of the monarchs beginning with Henry IV in 1589 and was coupled with a series of especially ruthless prime ministers. Men such as Richelieu and Mazarin wielded enormous power and left in their wake a well-ordered governmental structure ready-made for the absolutist training of Louis XIV. Louis XIV surrounded himself with capable advisers, military reformers, and financial experts. The net result was his personal control of the state exemplified by the palace complex at Versailles and France's commanding position in the European international order. The French wars of expansion in this era were meant to cap French glory but were thwarted by a combination of European states led by the Dutch United Provinces and ascendant England aligned against the threat. Political power, European hegemony, localized territorial gains, and religious attitudes were all factors in the four wars of Louis XIV. When these wars ended, France remained a great power, but a power no longer above Europe and one whose future, because of the Sun King's excesses, would soon be in doubt.

IDENTIFICATIONS

Identify each one of the following as used in the text. Refer to the text as necessary.

	Text Page
Millenary Petition	307
Duke of Buckingham	308-309
Petition of Right	308
Short Parliament	310
Grand Remonstrance	310
Cavaliers and Roundheads	311
"Pride's Purge"	312
Clarendon Code	313
English Bill of Rights of 1689	314
"one king, one law, one faith"	315
intendants	316
Fronde	317
Bishop Bossuet	319
Cornelius Jansen	321
mercantilism	321
Sebastien Vauban	322
Prince of Orange	323-325
Battle of Malplaquet	327
Peace of Utrecht-Rastadt	327

CHAPTER 13
PATHS TO
CONSTITUTIONALISM AND
ABSOLUTISM: ENGLAND AND
FRANCE IN THE
SEVENTEENTH CENTURY

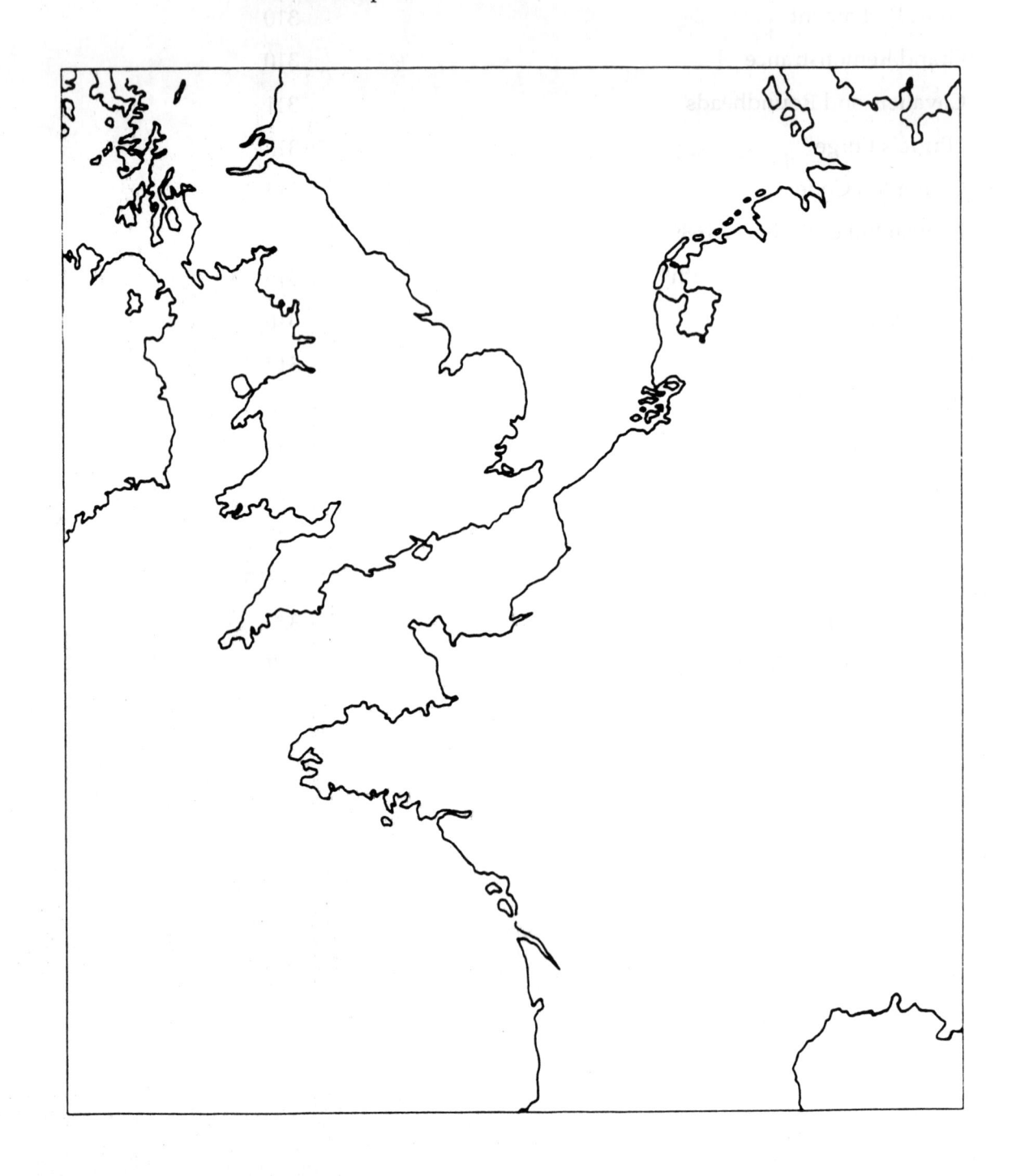

Map Exercise A

Locate each of the following areas on the accompanying map:

1. Irish Sea
2. English Channel
3. North Sea
4. Thames River
5. River Seine
6. Aix-la-Chapelle
7. Plymouth
8. Paris
9. Versailles
10. Nantes
11. Brussels
12. Utrecht
13. Amsterdam
14. Marston Moor
15. Naseby
16. Cambridge
17. London
18. Wales

MAP EXERCISE B

On this map of France, locate and mark each of the following areas and cities:

    RIVERS: Garonne, Loire, Rhone, Seine

    MOUNTAINS: Central Massif, Pyrenees, Vosges

    WATERS: Bay of Biscay, English Channel, Pas de Calais

    CITIES: Bordeaux, Cherbourg, La Rochelle, Le Havre, Lyons, Marseilles, Metz, Nancy, Nantes, Paris, Strasbourg, Tours, Versailles

CHAPTER 13
PATHS TO CONSTITUTIONALISM AND ABSOLUTISM: ENGLAND AND FRANCE IN THE SEVENTEENTH CENTURY

SHORT-ANSWER EXERCISES

Multiple-Choice

_____ 1. The book *A Trew Law of Free Monarchies* was written by: (a) James VI of Scotland, (b) John Locke, (c) Charles I, (d) Oliver Cromwell.

_____ 2. Early religious differences between James I and the Puritans fostered the founding of: (a) Puritannia, (b) Massachusetts Bay Colony, (c) Maryland, (d) New Amsterdam (New York).

_____ 3. Which of the following was least supportive of English monarchial government in the period 1620 through the 1640s: (a) Duke of Buckingham, (b) John Pym, (c) Thomas Wentworth, (d) William Laud.

_____ 4. The so-called Test Act was largely aimed at discrediting: (a) Titus Oates, (b) James, duke of York, (c) Charles II, (d) earl of Shaftesbury.

_____ 5. The reason for the continuing opposition to the reign of James II was his: (a) imprisonment of Anglican bishops, (b) appointments of known Catholics to high offices, (c) insistence upon the repeal of the Test Act, (d) all of these.

_____ 6. Which of the following was least directly responsible for the establishment of absolutism in France during the seventeenth century: (a) Louis XIII, (b) Sully, (c) Richelieu, (d) Mazarin.

_____ 7. Jansenists believed that: (a) human beings had been redeemed through Christ's death, (b) Cornelis Jansen should be canonized, (c) that human beings could not be redeemed without special grace from God, (d) St. Augustine had incorrectly interpreted the concept of original sin.

_____ 8. The marquis of Louvois is noted for all of the following except: (a) establishing a professional French army, (b) developing a system of trench warfare, (c) introducing a merit-based system of promotion, (d) increasing army pay.

_____ 9. Louis XIV considered the revocation of the Edict of Nantes as: (a) unimportant, (b) militarily significant, (c) his most pious act, (d) good for business.

_____ 10. The correct chronological order of these important treaties negotiated during the wars of Louis XIV would be: (a) Utrecht-Rastadt, Ryswick, Nijmwegen, (b) Nijmwegen, Ryswick, Utrecht-Rastadt, (c) Ryswick, Nijmwegen, Aix-la-Chapelle, (d) Nijmwegen, Utrecht-Rastadt, Ryswick.

True-False

_____ 1. John Pym's "proposed departure from tradition" involved the question of control of England's army.

_____ 2. The alliance with Scottish Presbyterians and the reorganization of the army under Parliament assured the Puritan victory over Charles I.

_____ 3. Charles II of England died a Roman Catholic.

_____ 4. The English Toleration Act of 1689 granted religious freedom to all but the most radical religious groups.

_____ 5. Despite his persecution of the Huguenots at home, Cardinal Richelieu allied France with Swedish Protestants during the Thirty Years' War.

_____ 6. Throughout the seventeenth century Catholic Jansenists allied with the Jesuits against French Huguenots.

_____ 7. Jean-Baptiste Colbert's economic policies had the effect of diminishing France's industrial and commercial potential.

_____ 8. In reality the revocation of the Edict of Nantes came as a complete surprise.

_____ 9. Philip of Anjou was the grandson of Louis XIV.

_____ 10. From a military perspective England's success in the War of Spanish Succession was the result of excellent leadership and superior weapons.

Completion

1. James VI of Scotland, who became James I of England, was the son of _____.

2. The religious minister under Charles I was _____ and in the 1630s he provoked a war with Scotland.

3. The largest military engagement of the English Civil War was the 1644 battle at _____.

4. The fate of Charles I appears to have been sealed when Cromwell's New Model Army defeated him at _____ in June 1645.

5. _____ was the official title used by Oliver Cromwell after taking power in 1653.

6. The so-called "Glorious Revolution" in England was justified in the work titled *Second Treatise on Government* written by _____.

7. Primarily to build and maintain roads, an involuntary labor force was created in France in the seventeenth century by the introduction of the _____.

8. Connecting the image of God to kings would be found in the writings of _____.

9. The most famous of the defenders of the Jansenist movement was _____.

10. _____ is the name used to describe the financial policies of the French minister Colbert.

FOR FURTHER CONSIDERATION

1. English politics during the seventeenth century was a blend of religious concerns and monarchial decline. How does the reign of Elizabeth I in the previous century set the stage for the struggle between king and Parliament in this era?

2. What factors do you consider important in assessing the success of the Puritans during Cromwell's era?

3. Assess the roles of Cardinals Richelieu and Mazarin in the establishment of absolutism in France.

4. Examine the reign of Louis XIV. What were his successes and what were his failures?

5. Compare and contrast the development of the governments of England and France during the seventeenth century. Answer with specific references to persons, statutes, and events as needed.

ANSWERS

Multiple-Choice

		Text Page
1.	A	307
2.	B	308
3.	B	309-310
4.	B	313
5.	D	314
6.	A	316
7.	C	321
8.	B	322
9.	C	325
10.	B	*passim*

True-False

1.	T	310
2.	T	311-312
3.	T	313
4.	F	314
5.	T	316
6.	F	321
7.	F	322
8.	F	324-325
9.	T	325
10.	T	325-326

Completion

1.	Mary Stuart, Queen of Scots	307
2.	William Laud	309
3.	Naseby	312
4.	Marston Moor	312
5.	Lord Protector	312
6.	John Locke	315
7.	*corveé*	315
8.	Bishop Bossuet	318
9.	Blaise Pascal	321
10.	Mercantilism	321

◆ ◆ ◆ ◆ ◆ ◆ ◆

NEW DIRECTIONS IN THOUGHT AND CULTURE IN THE SIXTEENTH AND SEVENTEENTH CENTURIES

COMMENTARY

It is clear today that the discoveries initiated in the sixteenth century have ever since profoundly influenced Western thought. From the beginning, examination of the universe, particularly the study of the earth and the sun, was opening an entire new world to the people of the late Renaissance. This study was pioneered by men like Copernicus and Galileo. Through them a medieval concept of learning, rooted in the Scholastic concentration on past achievements, was replaced by a forward-looking emphasis on nature. For the comparatively few intellectuals and writers of these centuries this change meant charting new courses, whether in literature, which sought to entertain, or philosophy, which sought to answer, or politics, which sought to act and explain. A new intellectual synthesis had to be formed.

However the changeover from a medieval to a modern view was not devoid of, and in fact spurred an era of vicious assault on those whose views could not be readily explained. Unquestionably these attacks upon suspected witches, the vast majority of whom were middle aged and older women, were stimulated by religious warfare and the uncertainties created by intellectual fermentation.

Almost all of these writers deserve careful attention. The scientists like Galileo, Brahe, and Kepler were to apply mathematical reasoning to their studies of nature and the universe. Galileo's telescope was an important breakthrough itself even though some skeptics refused to look through it. Others, like Descartes and Newton, attempted to take the mathematical models even further along the path of human understanding. In their respective quests for truth, Descartes attempted to get a fresh intellectual start by beginning with only his own existence, and Newton established the basis of modern physics.

Great volumes of nationalist literature also appeared at this time as contemporary writers felt freer than ever before to explore human nature in all its ramifications. Cervantes in Spain and Shakespeare in England were dominant influences in this category. Other writers, like Milton and Bunyan, clearly reflected the political-religious struggle in England at the time.

Philosophy was also affected. The new approaches to nature could not help but trigger questions about the nature of God. Pascal's work, for example, drew upon the earlier and comparatively conservative views of John Calvin and St. Augustine. Spinoza's emphasis on God as embracing all of nature became in part the basis of a new Humanist religion.

During the seventeenth century a basic and what turned out to be a far-reaching reexamination of political philosophy took place. The resultant views reflected the new earthbound rationalism initiated by these early modern scientists. Thomas Hobbes and

Chapter ◆ 14

John Locke, men of contrasting views, both lived through, and reflected on, turbulent political and religious times in England. Their works examined such basic concepts as the state of nature, the origin of state authority, and the social contract. As a result, their political works ever since have had a fundamental effect upon the political development of the West. Taken as a totality, these new intellectual directions brought to fruition and amplification ideas in science, technology, and philosophy that began with the Renaissance.

This Scientific Revolution, as it slowly unfolded for 150 years before the dawn of the eighteenth century, was an extensive and a most important development in the Western heritage.

IDENTIFICATIONS

Identify each one of the following as used in the text. Refer to text as necessary.

	Text Page
Scientific Revolution	330
Dialogues on the Two Chief Systems of the World	333
Principia Mathematica	335
malificium	336
"cunning folk"	336
Sancho Panza	338
William Shakespeare	339
Areopagitica	340
Paradise Lost	340
The Pilgrim's Progress	341
Discourse on Method	343
Pensées	344
Leviathan	345
"the desire for commodious living"	346
Anthony Ashley Cooper	346
Essay Concerning Human Understanding	347
Two Treatises on Government	347
Locke's "social contracts"	347

Map Exercise A

Using the Copernican model, mark each of the known planets in its correct orbit. Note each planet's distance from the sun.

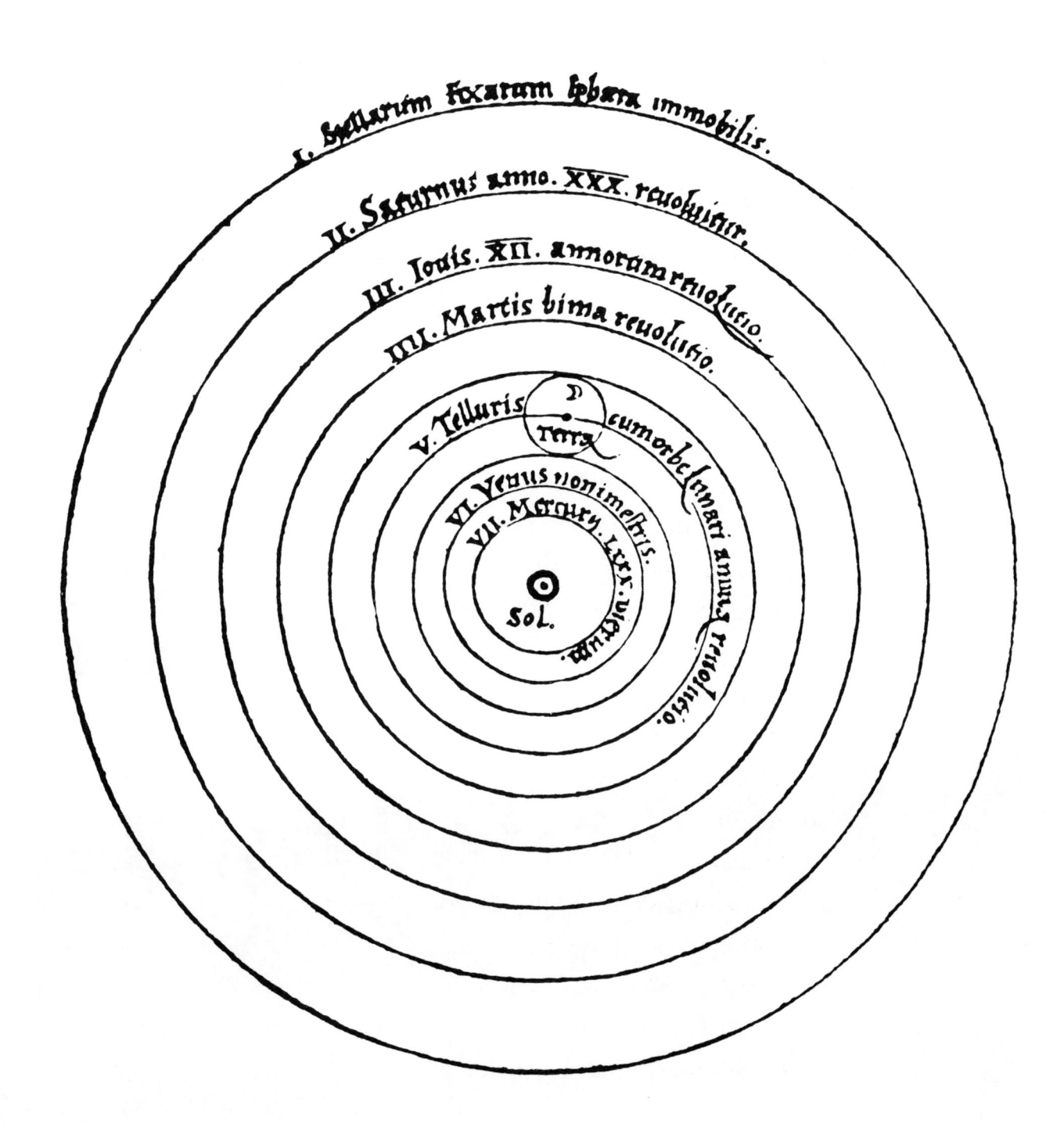

MAP EXERCISE B

In the approximately correct relationship to each other show the Sun, Earth, and the Moon. Indicate in miles and kilometers the exact distances between each. If possible, in days, how long would it take you to reach the Moon on a mountain bike, with a car, on a modern passenger jet, or a cruise ship?

Short-Answer Exercises

Multiple-Choice

_____ 1. Which of the following expressions best characterizes the nature of the Scientific Revolution? (a) it occurred several places in Europe at the same time, (b) it was not revolutionary in the normal sense of the word, (c) it grew out of the criticism associated with the Reformation, (d) all of these are correct.

_____ 2. Which of the following actually opposed Copernicus's views? (a) Tycho Brahe, (b) Johannes Kepler, (c) Galileo Galilei, (d) Francis Bacon.

_____ 3. The harmony between faith and science in this period is found in which of these views? (a) since nature is reasonable, God must be reasonable, (b) to study the laws of nature in reality is to study God, (c) faith and science are mutually supporting, (d) all of these.

_____ 4. During this era a classic argument for freedom of the press was written by: (a) Milton, (b) Shakespeare, (c) Cervantes, (d) Copernicus.

_____ 5. Which two of the following works most fervently expresses the idea of Puritan holiness? (a) *Grace Abounding*, (b) *Pilgrim's Progress*, (c) *Paradise Lost*, (d) *The Life and Death of Mr. Badman*.

_____ 6. Analytic geometry was first developed by: (a) Galileo, (b) Brahe, (c) Descartes, (d) none of these.

_____ 7. Pascal believed that: (a) there was danger in following traditional religious ways, (b) misery loves company, (c) God's mercy was for everyone, (d) it is better to believe in God than not to.

_____ 8. The most controversial thinker of the seventeenth century was: (a) René Descartes, (b) Blase Pascal, (c) Baruch Spinoza, (d) Thomas Hobbes.

_____ 9. In Thomas Hobbes's view, man was: (a) a person neither good nor evil, (b) a self-centered beast, (c) essentially God-fearing, (d) none of these.

_____ 10. Which of the following works was written first: (a) *On the Revolutions of Heavenly Spheres*, (b) *King Lear*, (c) *Leviathan*, (d) *Ethics*.

True-False

_____ 1. Nicolai Copernicus found the Ptolemaic system of the universe to be full of mathematical problems.

_____ 2. Middle aged and older women were particularly vulnerable during this era of witch hunts.

_____ 3. Don Quixote, Dulcinea, and Sancho Panza are all characters in Miguel de Cervantes' masterpiece.

Completion

1. The Ptolemaic view of the universe is found in a work written in the second century and titled the _____.

2. The work of _____ expanded on the previous efforts of Nicolaus Copernicus and Tycho Brahe.

3. For Galileo the rationality for the entire universe was based on _____.

4. The power of the Catholic Church and the Inquisition largely prevented the Protestant Reformation from coming to _____.

5. As a young man, _____ was decorated for gallantry in the great naval battle of Lepanto.

6. The author of the story in which the characters journey to the Celestial City is _____.

7. Perfecting the microscope is usually associated with the work of _____ and _____.

8. The political philosopher Thomas Hobbes believed that the dangers of _____ were greater than the dangers of tyranny.

9. _____ was the author of *Patriarcha, or the Natural Power of Kings*.

10. _____ believed that human ruling went beyond control of the jungle of selfish egomaniacs; it required the ruler to preserve the law of nature.

For Further Consideration

1. Describe the roles of Nicolaus Copernicus and Francis Bacon in influencing what is now referred to as the Scientific Revolution.

2. What was the new world view worked out during this era? How did it differ from the medieval view? What effects did the new concept of the universe have on all of the sciences?

FOR FURTHER CONSIDERATION

1. Describe the roles of Nicolaus Copernicus and Francis Bacon in influencing what is now referred to as the Scientific Revolution.

2. What was the new world view worked out during this era? How did it differ from the medieval view? What effects did the new concept of the universe have on all of the sciences?

3. How were the lives of Miguel de Cervantes and William Shakespeare different? What effect did their experiences have on their writing? Cite specific examples.

4. Discuss the central characteristics of the thought of Thomas Hobbes. Are there parts of his work that are reflected in modern times?

5. Contrast Hobbes's view of authority with that of John Locke. Why is Locke considered so influential even in modern times?

Answers

CHAPTER 14
NEW DIRECTIONS IN
THOUGHT AND CULTURE IN
THE SIXTEENTH AND
SEVENTEENTH CENTURIES

Multiple-Choice

		Text Page
1.	D	330-333
2.	A	331
3.	D	335
4.	A	340
5.	A and B	341
6.	C	343
7.	D	344
8.	C	344
9.	B	346
10.	A	*passim*

True-False

1.	T	331
2.	T	337
3.	T	338
4.	F	339
5.	T	340
6.	T	341
7.	F	343
8.	T	344
9.	F	345
10.	T	346

Completion

1.	*Almagest*	330
2.	Johannes Kepler	332
3.	mathematics	333
4.	Spain	338
5.	Miguel de Cervantes	338
6.	John Bunyan	341
7.	Robert Hooke/ Anton von Leeuwenhoek	342
8.	anarchy	346
9.	Sir Robert Filmer	347
10.	John Locke	347

◆◆◆◆◆◆◆

Chapter 15

SUCCESSFUL AND UNSUCCESSFUL PATHS TO POWER (1686-1740)

COMMENTARY

The end of the seventeenth and the early part of the eighteenth century were a period of state building. While perhaps not in the modern sense of nation building, wherein the role of the ordinary citizen would become a factor, it was in the sense of building the state organizational structure. The role of an increasingly international economy and empire building in the Americas contributed to the necessity of new infrastructures. The Reformation itself, the religiously inspired warfare that followed, and such great wars as the Thirty Years' War (1618-1648) and the Great Northern War (1700-1721), clearly undermined the medieval nature of state systems. The intellectual achievements of the so-called Scientific Revolution had profoundly altered views on how states might be governed. The initial decades of the eighteenth century provided an opportunity for states to catch up on their own internal development. At the same time the stage was being set for more dramatic changes at the end of the century.

As a result of internal reforms, certain Western European states were placed on the road to modernity whereas other states languished by the end of the century. England was to remain in the forefront of political and economic development, while in Brandenburg-Prussia (the future Germany) and in the Russia of Peter the Great important steps would be taken that would have far-reaching impact on both nations' future development. Within the general framework of change in governmental structure and reform several distinct developments were taking place.

The positions of Spain and the Netherlands would wane in the eighteenth century. In France the absolutism so ruthlessly established in the previous century would be streamlined, and though corrupted, would remain well entrenched in the French system. In England the influence of Parliament would grow, placing that country on the road to liberal reform and, ultimately, to industrial growth. Further eastward in Europe, nations appeared to be developing modern state systems largely through the dominating personalities of monarchs like Frederick William, the Great Elector of Prussia, his son Frederick William I, and Peter the Great of Russia. Despite the efforts of the Hapsburg emperor of Austria, Charles VI, his lack of a male successor to the throne weakened that ancient Catholic monarchy. Russian entrance into the European arena reflected the troubled and often ambivalent relationship that nation had maintained with Western states for centuries. This era witnessed a decline of Sweden, Poland, and the Ottoman Empire. Notable also during this era was the increasing importance of overseas empires that served to support their "mother" states in Europe. In empire-building, too, at least for a time, France and England would enjoy a distinct advantage.

More clearly, by the mid-eighteenth century several of the European states were destined for second-class status, whereas others, because of a confluence of factors, were able to better themselves. Although these developments did not reach a climax in this era, the world stage was being set for a great power struggle in the period from 1750 through the age of Napoleon, ending in 1815.

IDENTIFICATIONS

Identify each one of the following as used in the text. Refer to the text as necessary.

	Text Page
John Law	351
parlements	352
South Sea Company	354
"Let sleeping dogs lie"	354
Great Northern War	357
zimmis	358
"exploding" the Diet	359
Magyars	359
Pragmatic Sanction	360
The Great Elector	361-363
Junkers	361
Frederick William I	363
"Time of Troubles"	364
Mikhail Romanov	364
boyers and *streltsy*	364-466
Table of Ranks	366
Old Believers Movement	366
Saint Petersburg	367

MAP EXERCISE A

Locate and mark the boundaries of those states that border the Austrian Empire.

Trace the Danube River through the Austrian Empire.

Locate each of the following cities:

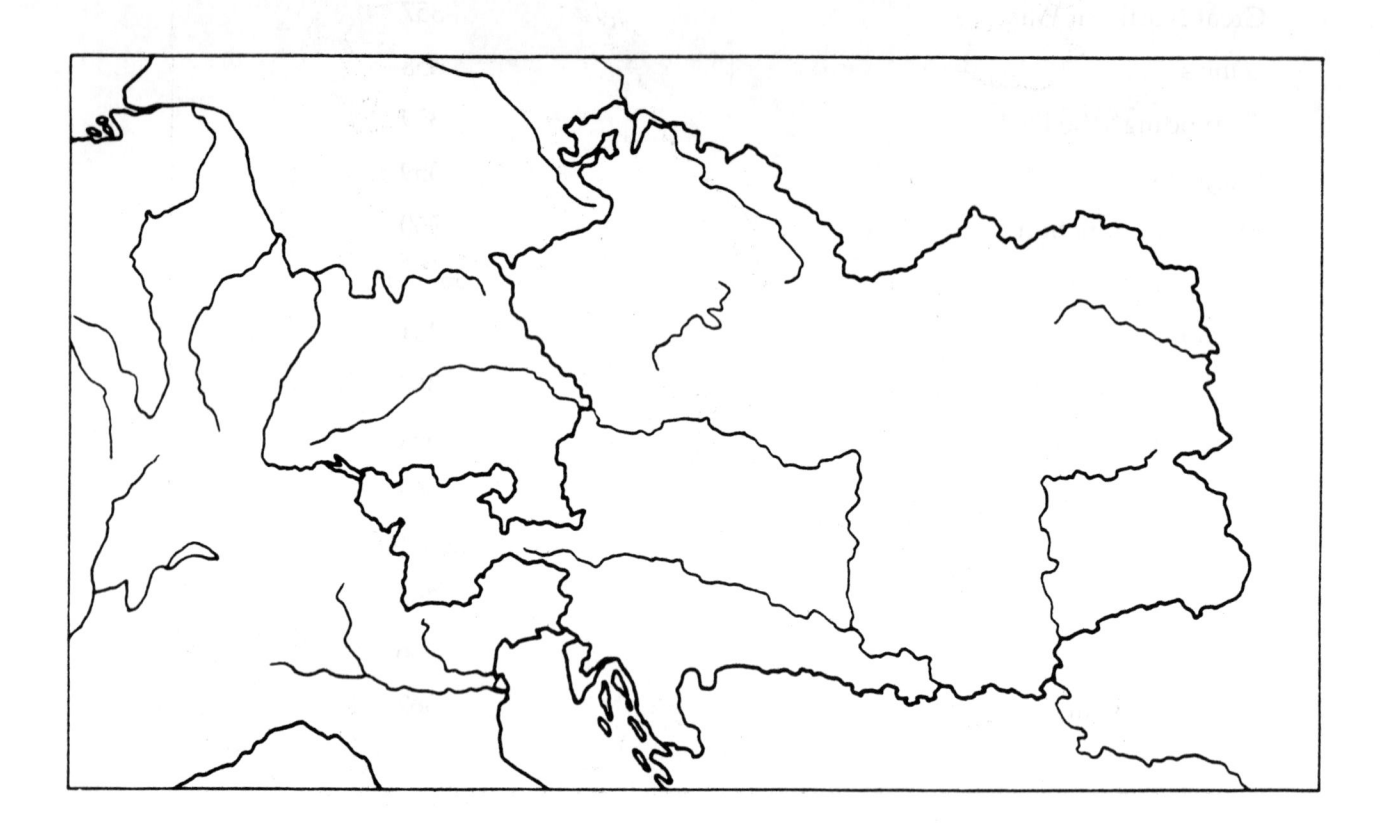

1. Vienna
2. Budapest
3. Prague
4. Lemberg
5. Belgrade
6. Mohacs

MAP EXERCISE B

Outline each of the following countries/areas: Sweden, Finland and Russia.

Locate the cities of Stockholm, St. Petersburg, Moscow, and Helsinki.

Ma ' the Baltic Sea, Lake Ladoga, and the Gulf of Finland.

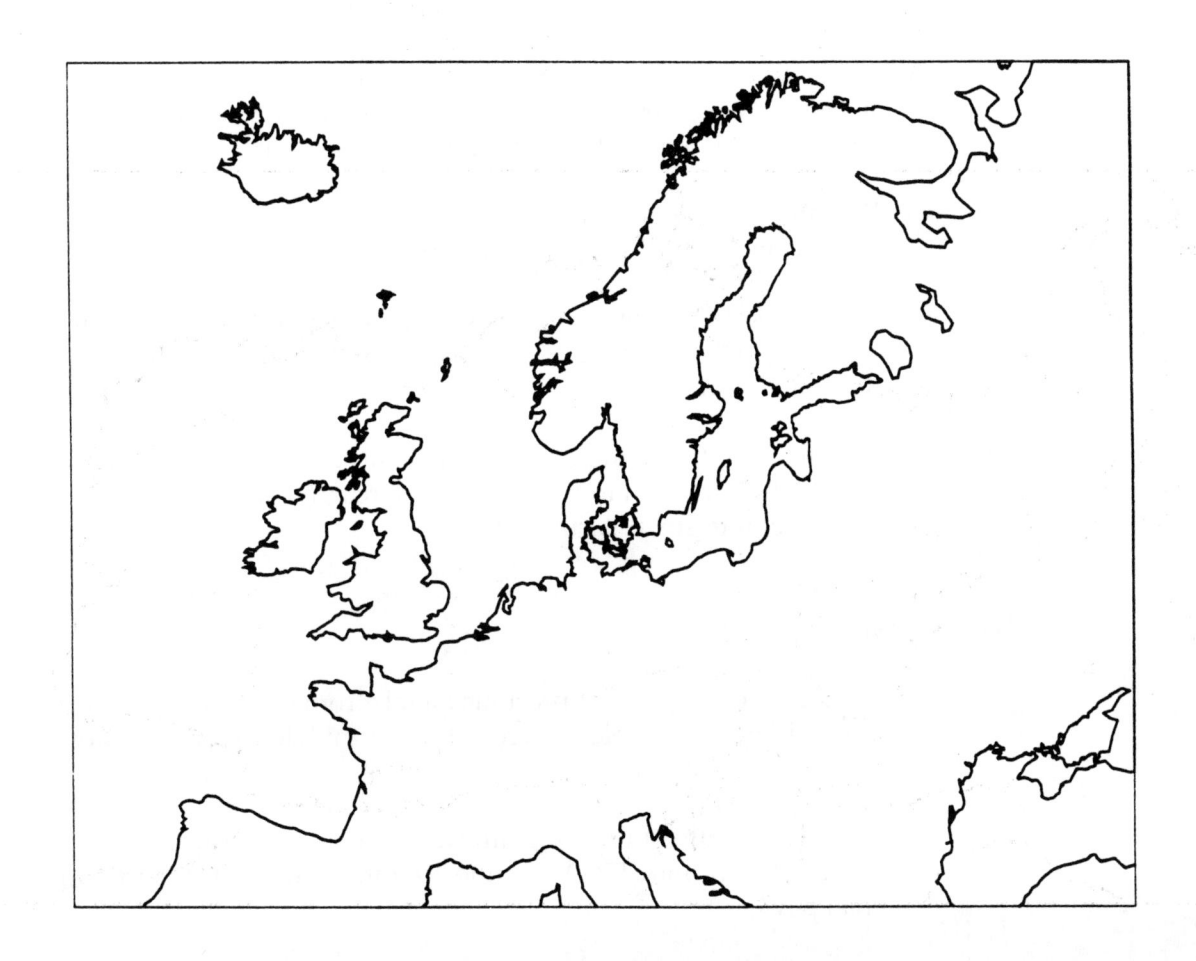

SHORT-ANSWER EXERCISES

Multiple-Choice

____ 1. According to the text, which of the following countries was not moving forward in this period? (a) Great Britain, (b) Russia, (c) Spain, (d) Prussia.

____ 2. Which of the following contributed *least* to the decline of the Netherlands in the eighteenth century? (a) the fishing industry, (b) shipbuilding, (c) the financial community, (d) various domestic industries.

____ 3. The Mississippi Company: (a) after earlier troubles operated profitably, (b) was responsible for the management of the French national debt, (c) ended the financial career of John Law, (d) all of these.

_____ 4. During the eighteenth century the English Parliament was dominated by: (a) the old aristocracy, (b) the rising middle class, (c) owners of property, (d) representatives of the people.

_____ 5. As one moved farther eastward in Europe in the eighteenth century there was increasing likelihood of finding: (a) rotten boroughs, (b) serfdom, (c) prominent intellectuals, (d) larger navies.

_____ 6. During this period of time Sweden's weakness was in her: (a) economy, (b) army, (c) location on the Baltic Sea, (d) none of these.

_____ 7. In the early eighteenth century a major defeat of Sweden occurred in the battle of: (a) Poltava, (b) Regensburg, (c) Narva, (d) none of these.

_____ 8. Beginning in this era a major factor in European international relations was the decline of: (a) the Ottoman Empire, (b) Poland, (c) Russia, (d) Austria.

_____ 9. The General-Ober-Finanz-Kriegs-und-Domänen-Direktorium is normally associated with the state of: (a) Russia, (b) Poland, (c) Prussia, (d) the Holy Roman Empire.

_____ 10. Which of the following occurred first? (a) Russia defeated in the battle at Narva, (b) European tour of Peter the Great, (c) Saint Petersburg founded, (d) end of the Great Northern War.

True-False

_____ 1. By relying on imports of precious metals from the New World the government of Spain was able to successfully stimulate that nation's overall economic development.

_____ 2. The chief feature of French political life in the eighteenth century until the French Revolution (1789) was the attempt of the nobility to limit monarchial power.

_____ 3. Louis XV of France is considered a failure not only because of his mediocrity but that he was never properly trained as a ruler, was lazy and given to vice.

_____ 4. Both Whigs and Tories were proponents of the status quo in England, yet the Tories supported urban commercial interests and were in favor of religious toleration in general.

_____ 5. Robert Walpole's success resulted from his careful use of government patronage and manipulation of the House of Commons.

_____ 6. By the end of the seventeenth century, warfare and the resultant shifting political loyalties had become basic ingredients of life in central Europe.

_____ 7. The Pragmatic Sanction was designed to insure the succession to the Austrian throne of Maria Theresa.

_____ 8. Frederick II (Hohenzollern) of Prussia married Maria Theresa (Habsburg) of Austria to insure his title to the lands of Prussia.

_____ 9. As a result of frequent revolutions, military conspiracies, and assassinations the Romanov's only ruled Russia for 100 years.

_____ 10. By the middle of the eighteenth century Russia was Europe's largest producer of iron.

Completion

1. The Treaty of _____ established a French interest in the Spanish monarchy.

2. Though not having the power to legislate, the _____ of France became effective centers of resistance to royal authority.

3. The most influential minister in the reign of France's Louis XV was the aged _____.

4. In reality _____ could be considered the first Prime Minister of Great Britain.

5. By laying siege to the city of _____ in 1683 the Turks were able to demonstrate the power of the Ottoman Empire.

6. The *liberum veto* was a practice exercised in the central legislative assembly of _____.

7. The rise of the Hohenzollern family to control of Prussia began with their rule of the German territory of _____.

8. _____ were the important class of German nobility influential throughout Prussian history.

9. In 1722 Peter the Great attempted to rearrange the Russian nobility through the _____.

10. An early attempt at religious reform in Russia was led by the Patriarch _____.

FOR FURTHER CONSIDERATION

1. Describe the development of parliamentary government in England in the first half of the eighteenth century. What kind of compromises made this unique system work?

2. Looking at the history of the Ottoman Empire (modern Turkey), what does the text see as the causes of the "political and ethnic turmoil that still continues" to this day?

3. How does the development of central authority in Prussia differ from that in other European states during this period? How was it similar?

4. Why were the so-called "reform" efforts of Russia's Peter the Great successful only in part?

5. Generally characterize the differences between the Eastern European States [Sweden, Poland, Austria, Prussia, and Russia] and the Western states [France and England].

ANSWER

Multiple-Choice

			Text Page
1.	C		349
2.	C		351
3.	D		351
4.	C		354
5.	B		357
6.	A		357
7.	A		357
8.	A		358
9.	C		363
10.	B		365

True-False

1.	F		350
2.	T		352
3.	T		352
4.	F		353
5.	T		354
6.	T		357
7.	T		360
8.	F		361
9.	F		364
10.	T		367

Completion

1.	Utrecht	350
2.	*parlements*	352
3.	Cardinal Fleury	352
4.	Robert Walpole	354
5.	Vienna	358
6.	Poland	359
7.	Brandenburg	361
8.	Junkers	361-362
9.	Table of Ranks	366
10.	Nikon	366

❖ ❖ ❖ ❖ ❖ ❖ ❖

FOR FURTHER CONSIDERATION OF THE DOCUMENTS

Each of the following questions is designed to help you reach a better understanding of the original documents presented in the last five chapters of the text. Feel free to use the page numbers provided to refer back to the document as necessary. The value of a primary historical source should not be underestimated; it helps us understand the nature of the era in which it was written.

Luther on Justification by Faith (p. 258)
1. Explain what is being "justified?" How does Luther arrive at "faith alone?" What are your views on Luther and eternity?

The Right to Resist Tyranny (p. 287)
2. Though more often stated in later centuries, Theodore Beza touches upon a basic premise respective to the origin of authority within a state which is fundamental to Western political thought. Explain this premise fully.

Bossuet on the Divine Right of Kings (p. 318)
3. What was the basis of Bossuet's defense of the concept of divine right? What are your views on the origin of government authority?

Galileo Discusses Science and the Bible (pp. 332-333)
4. How do Galileo's arguments hold up in light of similar debates today which center around the role of God in the world, particularly since Darwin (1859)?

Lady Montagu's Advice on Election to Parliament (p. 356)
5. What does this letter suggest about the role of women of high birth in the eighteenth century?